THE COCKER SPANIEL

Alpheus of Dorswick   Sixshot Black Swan

Sh. Ch. Sixshot Woodywoodpecker

THE
COCKER SPANIEL

VERONICA LUCAS-LUCAS

ARCO PUBLISHING COMPANY, INC.

New York

Published in the United States
by ARCO PUBLISHING COMPANY, Inc.
219 Park Avenue South, New York, N.Y. 10003
Copyright © Veronica Lucas-Lucas 1959, 1964 and 1967
Chapter VIII © Popular Dogs Publishing Co. Ltd 1967

First published in U.S.A. 1970

Library of Congress Catalogue Number 76–97946
Standard Book Number 668–02160–8

Printed in Great Britain

ACKNOWLEDGMENTS

The line drawing illustrating the Standard of the Cocker on page 37 is reproduced by kind permission of the Cocker Spaniel Club and the pedigree of Ch. Invader of Ware on pages 24 and 25 is reproduced with the kind permission of the late Mr. H. S. Lloyd.

COCKER LOVE

There's a love that lingers always
Deep within my heart—
It's the love for cocker spaniels,
Here's how it got its start.
Bought a puppy, silky-coated,
Eyes of brown that looked at me
Like he thought I was an idol,
Showed his trust and faith in me.
Stubby tail that wagged "Hello, there!"
Every time he heard my step
Fitted his mood right with my moods,—
Quiet, or a lot of pep.
Ears that gracefully extended
Quite a ways toward the ground—
Chasing after balls; retrieving
Anything he found around.
Gentle always with the children
As he grew from puppyhood
Into just the kind of dog folks
Liked throughout the neighbourhood.
I'm a hunter and I love it,
So did that first cocker pup—
Didn't really have to train him,
He just seemed to pick it up.
Years have passed, but still that puppy
In my heart has left his trace,
For every time I lose a cocker
Another one must take its place.

VERA PAGE.

CONTENTS

8   CONTENTS

CHAPTER VII

CHAPTER VIII

APPENDIX

ILLUSTRATIONS

9

AUTHOR'S INTRODUCTIONS

I have written this book chiefly for the novice, and hope it will be of some little help, and save him from making the many mistakes I made when I began breeding and showing. It is written in simple language for the benefit of everyone who keeps or intends to keep a cocker as a show dog or pet, and who, it is hoped, will each find in it information of practical value. Readers who have no knowledge of the origin and ancestry of the cocker will, I trust, find the description I have given enlightening.

The close association I have had with cockers has naturally led to a keen interest in their development and welfare. I have always loved the cocker spaniel since my childhood days. We lived in the country and my father had quite a variety of gun-dogs, but they were not show dogs and were kept entirely for the gun.

My favourite was always the little cocker and when I left home I took one with me. He missed his companions so much that I decided to buy a little bitch puppy to keep him company. It so happened I chose one from an "Of Ware" sire. She not only turned out to be a winner, but was the basis of my strain; from her I bred Sixshot Bunting, who was mated to Woodcock Othello (full brother to Treetops Treasure Trove) and out of this mating came Sixshot Ring Ouzel, who did a lot of good winning, including best black bitch at Cruft's. I then mated Ouzel to Woodcock Ringleader and this mating produced Sixshot Mavis, who also did a lot of winning and afterwards became Treetops Temptress, the dam of Treetops Turtle Dove. I had previously mated Mavis to Bazel Otto and from this mating came the famous red bitch Sixshot Brown Owl who, when mated to Treetops Terrific, produced one of the most famous black dogs ever, Sixshot Black Swan. He in turn sired Sixshot Willy Wagtail who, when mated to Sixshot Nightingale, produced Sh. Ch. Sixshot Woodywood-pecker. The dogs I have mentioned above are the ones which will be remembered by cocker breeders.

I would like to thank the kind friends in the following list for helping me with pedigrees, dates, etc.: Mr. H. S. Lloyd, Judge

Townsend Scudder (U.S.A.), Mr. Frank Williams, Mr. H. C. Wicks, Miss M. Barker (New Zealand). Mr. P. R. A. Moxon, who must be recognized as one of our great authorities on the training of gundogs, has kindly written a Chapter on *The Cocker Spaniel as a Gundog*, which is a very pleasing addition. The Chapter on the Treatment of Diseases has been read by a veterinary surgeon.

1953

In this new edition I have made some additions to the text and introduced several new kennels in Chapter II and new C.C. winners in Chapter V. New photographs of recent Certificate winners have also been included.

1956

For this third edition, Chapters II and V have again been revised and a list of British Cocker Champions and Show Champions from 1948 to 1958 has been added as an appendix. I have also taken the opportunity of bringing the illustrations up-to-date by including photographs of some Cockers which are now being successfully shown.

1959

There is little for me to add to the fourth edition as what I wrote in the first instance still stands. A few new photographs now appear; where necessary the text has been revised, and Chapters II and V have again been brought up-to-date, as has the appendix.

1964

I was very pleased to be asked to revise this book once again. I have made cuts in matter that is now out of date and made certain additions; four photographs have been replaced and the appendix brought up-to-date. Mr. F. Andrew Edgson, MRCVS has kindly contributed an entirely fresh chapter on Some Commoner Health Problems. With these alterations the fifth edition is launched under the new title of *The Cocker Spaniel*.

V. L.-L.

1967

Sh. Ch. Astrawin Amusing

Ch. Broomleaf Bonny Lad
of Shillwater

Sh. Ch. Sixshot Dan the Duck

Merryworth Molasses,
aged 10 months

Harley Gayson

Sh. Ch. Bonny Lass of Kenavon

Sixshot Gobble the Turkey

Sixshot the Black Cockatoo

CHAPTER I

EARLY HISTORY OF THE COCKER SPANIEL

THE cocker spaniel is always a merry little dog at work or play.
At all times he shows his pleasure by the continual wag of his
tail, and he is never so happy as when putting up game for the
guns, or retrieving a fallen bird from land, water or hedgerow.
How far the spaniel goes back in history would be hard to say, but
it has been mentioned in early writings as far back as the 14th
century. In the early days all breeds of spaniels came under one
heading, "Spaniels". The name "cocker" or "cocking spaniel"
came into being about 1800. At this period they were used a great
deal for woodcock shooting, being able to work through dense
cover where one of the larger breeds could not penetrate. The
name of the cocker was registered at the Kennel Club in 1893.
Until the year 1901 the weight limit was 25 lb., but in this year
the limit was abolished by the Spaniel Club on a resolution
proposed by Colonel Cane, seconded by Mr. James Farrow and
confirmed by the Kennel Club. This gave the breeders more
scope. Before this a spaniel could be a cocker, and if he put on
weight he became a springer; in other words, dogs from the
same litter could be of two different classes: under 25 lb. cockers
and over 25 lb. springers.

THE SPANIEL IN FALCONRY

The popularity of the cocker spaniel is world-wide, no doubt
due to his versatility. The answer will be found in the fact that
he has several strings to his bow, being equally suitable as a
gundog, showman or companion. In the time of the Stuarts he
was used for Falconry, a sport indulged in largely on the Fens, and
enjoyed by the leaders of venery and fashion in Europe; this was
at its zenith in England during the reign of Charles II. I think it

might be of interest at this point to quote George Tumberville who, in his *Booke of Faulconorie*, published in 1575, wrote "Howe necessary a thing a spanell is to Falconrie." This goes to prove that even in those very early days the spaniel was a sporting dog.

John Evelyn. "Stonehenge"

In the 14th century Chaucer mentions a spaniel in *The Wyf of Bathes Prologue*. About 200 years later, in 1570, Dr. Cains wrote, in his history of the *Englishe Dogges* that the "Spaniell whose skynnes are white, and if marcked with any spottes they are commonly red . . ." Another writer of this period, John Evelyn, records in his diary, on July 8th, 1647, at La Charite, "I lost my faithful spaniel Piccoli who had followed me from Rome, it seems he had been taken up by some of the Governor's pages or footmen without recovery, which was a great displeasure to me." In a fifth edition of *The Dogs of British Islands*, published in 1888, "Stonehenge" wrote: "The modern Field spaniel should be the best made all round shooting dog, for he is expected to perform equally well on land and in water, in covert, hedgerow or turnips. He is also called on to return whilst he must be thoroughly steady, reliable under all circumstances, however trying to his nature, and he must never tire." In order to attain this marvellous combination of powers and varied qualifications our modern breeders have crossed the old-fashioned cocker with the Sussex, and then by careful selection as to size, points and colour they have established a breed. Thus we learn that before 1886 the blood of the Sussex variety of spaniels had been added to the cocker admixture of bloods of other varieties of spaniels, and it was producing what "Stonehenge" characterized as "A marvellous combination of powers and varied qualifications." In the early days, a strain of working cockers was bred in Devonshire, which were hardy and good with the gun, and all along the Devon coast you would find many of these little dogs, eager to accompany any sportsman on a day's shooting, although they were not good retrievers on the whole, which perhaps was just as well as these dogs turned out by the dozen. Their breeding was not studied, except by a few, and yet they seemed to follow a certain type; the principal colours were blue and liver roans, liver and white, and the solids were chiefly liver, with a few reds.

COCKERS IN DEVONSHIRE

I remember in recent years attending a shooting party in Devonshire; with a full gale blowing a cock pheasant shot coming down wind had fallen across water. All the dogs had refused to go across, but one little cocker bitch unhesitatingly swam the water, and brought back the bird. This was the best retrieve I had ever seen with a dog of this size.

EARLY BREEDING

The founder of the modern cocker was Mr. James Farrow, who did so much towards the standardization of the breed with his original OBO, who was cocker bred for several generations, and later by OBO's great-grandsire Champion Ted OBO, who was by Frank OBO out of Champion Lily OBO. Mr. Isaac Sharpe made history for cockers when the first field trials in this country, confined to all spaniels, was run at Sutton Scarsdale in 1889. The stake was won with the cocker Stylish Pride owned by Mr. Sharpe. The first cocker to qualify as a Field Trial Champion was Colonel Heseltone's Field Trial Champion Walhampton Judy, who was sired by Champion Rufus Bowdler out of Jum Jum and bred by Mr. A. E. Halsey in 1905, trained and handled by Mr. John Kent. It was a great event for the cocker spaniel in 1909 when Mr. Phillips's Rivington Robena obtained her working qualifying certificate in the field as well as obtaining three show Challenge Certificates, thus making her a full champion.

FOUNDATION OF THE COCKER SPANIEL CLUB

A milestone in history was made when the Cocker Spaniel Club was formed in 1902 by a few enthusiastic breeders and from then onwards great steps have been made towards the betterment of the cocker. After the First World War the cocker spaniel really came into its own, and mostly tops entries over all breeds at the championship shows. In the year 1914 only 400 registrations were made at the Kennel Club but in 1939 the registration figure jumped to 5,372 and in 1947 the peak figure of 27,000 was reached.

This goes to show how popular the cocker spaniel has become and how this little dog has captured the hearts of so many; he is undoubtedly a staunch favourite, as the registration figure exceeds any other breed by thousands.

Mr. Rawdon B. Lee in "Modern Dogs"

I have read with great interest the Chapter written on the cocker spaniel by Mr. Rawdon B. Lee in *Modern Dogs* in the year 1897 and thought it would be of interest to cocker enthusiasts to transcribe some of the Chapter. Mr. Rawdon Lee had a very poor opinion of the cocker as a show dog, and also as a gundog, which makes rather amusing reading, as it is quite contradictory to what has really happened, when we think of the cocker of today, usually topping entries at all the championship shows and the highest registration at the Kennel Club, and to see him work is a joy. I have often been amazed to see a cocker bringing to hand a struggling wounded rabbit or cock pheasant. Most cockers have the ability to work, but unfortunately so few of us have the space or time to train them, therefore their natural instinct as a gundog is lost. Cockers are fortunately adaptable little creatures and are equally happy as a companion.

An extract on the cocker spaniel from *Modern Dogs* written as mentioned above:

"This, the smallest of our race of sporting spaniels, is retrograding rather than progressing, and hardy, cheerful little dog though he be, sportsmen have found that a bigger dog can do his duties better, even to working rough covert, and it is not a general thing for a cocker to retrieve a rabbit or a hare; indeed, some cockers I have had would not retrieve at all, nor did I blame them, for retrieving is a duty to be performed by a more powerful dog. The prizes offered for the cocker on the show bench are not of particular value, nor do they carry sufficient honour, to make it worth the while of anyone breeding him for such purpose alone, so as a matter of fact, this once-favoured little dog is not growing with the times in the manner which savours of success. Only the larger exhibitions give him classes of his own, and the prizes then do not always go to the genuine article. The cocker of the olden time I should take to be the connecting link between the working and the toy spaniels. We have been told that the Blenheims at Marlborough House were excellent dogs to work the coverts for cock and pheasant, and excepting in colour there is in reality not much difference in appearance between the older orange and white toys (not as they are today, with their abnormally short noses, round skulls and enormous eyes) and the liver and white cockers H. B. Chalon drew for Daniel's *Rural Sports* in 1801. Two of Chalon's little spaniels have just sprung a woodcock, and charming specimens they are, not too low on the leg, nor overdone in the matter of ears, but sprightly little dogs, evidently under 20 lb. weight and of a type we do not find today. Many of us lament the growing scarcity of this variety as he was to be found fifty years ago and more. Modern breeders tell us they have provided us with a better and handsomer animal. It is an open question whether they have done the former; I acknowledge they have done the latter. Some few years ago I became the possessor of a brace of black cockers, the most beautiful little spaniels imaginable. How they were bred I am not aware; this I do know, that wherever they went they were admired more than any other dogs; not in the show ring—they never appeared there—but in the streets and the country generally. At that time I was shooting a good deal, and had ample opportunity of entering them to game of every kind. As sporting dogs they were comparatively useless, for they were noisy, headstrong, not at all careful, and would pass half a dozen rabbits or pheasants whilst they were putting up three or four. My terriers could beat their heads off, and a cross bred spaniel I had at that time could have outworked a big team of them. Of course, this must not be taken as an implication that all these modern extremely pretty black cockers are equally useless, but from others I have seen at work I did not take mine to have been an especially unfortunate brace.

"The coats of some of them are not adapted to protect the hide of the dog from being pierced by those sharp thorns and prickly brambles that are to be found in every ordinary covert.

"Some parts of Wales and Devonshire have produced the old working type of cocker, mostly liver and white in colour, higher on the leg than an ordinary field spaniel, not so long in ears, with a close coat, not too fine, usually inclining to be wavy and curly on the hindquarters, and a head finer in the muzzle than the ordinary spaniel would seem to possess, and with a character of its own. About twenty-five years ago Dr. Boulton was exhibiting his Rhea, a black specimen which won a great many prizes. She, however, had little or no strain of the cocker in her, and what excellence she possessed came from the same blood that ran in the pedigree of Bullock's Nellie and other celebrities of her day.

"Perhaps the best class of cockers I have ever seen was benched at Manchester in 1892. There were fourteen of them, of many types, but amongst them specimens of both the old and modern style. Mr. H. J. Price of Long Ditton had an excellent team, his Ditton Brevity and Gaiety being particularly excellent, the one a blue and white, the other a tricolour. Mr. Carew-Gibson of Fareham, in Grove Rose and Merry Belle, had a brace of beauties, also of the old type, and his first-named won chief prize; but other leading honours of third and reserve were given to miniature modern spaniels, both black, but certainly not like Rose and Brevity, that took first and second honours. Mr. Phillips's Rivington Merry Legs was another of the pure strain, a black and white that I believe came from Exeter; and at the most recent Manchester show, that in 1897, the latter exhibitor benched a brace of beauties, Rivington Bee and Sue by Bruton Victor Busy, which won leading honours in their group.

"I have particularly drawn attention to these classes at Manchester in proof, if such were needed, that there still remains material in the country to popularize the old-fashioned breed of cocker and I fancy this would soon be done would judges, in making their awards, stick to one type and throw out those dogs that showed unusually heavy bone, long bodies, heavy heads and over-sized ears. And I may go further than this and say that I never yet saw a good and perfectly characteristic cocker that had a flat coat, was entirely black, or of that bright liver colour found in the Sussex. The correct colours are a mixed roan, or a dull brown and white, or black and white and brown, but the latter have white on the chest and often enough white feet also. Mr. J. F. Farrow of Ipswich owns an excellent strain of small black spaniels, one or two of which are of the cocker type of which I approve. Some of them are miniature specimens of the black field spaniel, and from which they are bred, but his Frank OBO, Ted OBO, and Lily OBO are quite of the correct old-fashioned type. Mr. J. W. Caless, Shipston-on-Stour, Mr. H. Singleton, Leamington Spa, Miss F. Canham, Forest Gate, own some of the best specimens of the day, their Brutus, Floss, Ladas, and Liko

Joko usually winning when they appear in the ring. In weight the cocker ought not to exceed 25 lb. at the very most and bitches 20 lb. or less are the desirable size. As I have already hinted, they should not be so high on the leg, so long in the body, so heavy in the ears, or so heavy in the muzzle as an ordinary field spaniel, and may be taken as sharp, active little creatures, always busy when at work, and especially smart in driving rabbits from a gorse covert or other rough place."

THE COCKER AND THE STAGE

The cocker has also achieved success on the stage. Tuppenny of Ware made a name for himself in *The Barretts of Wimpole Street* at the Queen's Theatre, London, and whilst on tour Lupin of Ware and Restless of Ware made a great hit in the same part. When the film version was remade in 1957 by M.G.M., John Holmes's Flush appeared in the role.

Among our English novelists none appears to be such a great lover of the cocker as John Galsworthy, whose black cocker spaniel is commemorated in a delightfully illustrated book, *Memories*. The character of the cocker named John in the novel *The Country House* is one of the finest studies of a dog in our English literature.

THE KENNEL CLUB

The high standard the cocker spaniel has attained in the British Isles has been made possible by the Kennel Club, which was founded in April 1873. Their first home was Victoria Street, Westminster, but the headquarters at the present time is 1-4 Clarges Street, London, W.1. The first recognized show was held in 1873 and very soon after this a stud-book was started. They then brought in a rule that no dog could be exhibited at any show under the jurisdiction of the Kennel Club without it being registered. About this time they began publishing the *Kennel Gazette*, which includes a record of registrations, transfers, and all matters dealing with dogs. All these steps help to insure the dog world against the fraudulent exhibitor and breeder, and anyone found guilty of discreditable conduct in a matter arising out of dogs is rightly suspended from exhibiting or registering a dog.

The Kennel Club has in its possession trophies worth several thousand pounds, many of which are for competition annually. The work of the Kennel Club is of the greatest importance to the canine world and as a governing body their responsibility cannot be over-estimated.

The Kennel Club held its first own show at the Crystal Palace in 1873 and has continued it ever since with the exception of the breaks necessitated by the two world wars.

The following is a list of the number of Cocker Spaniels registered anually at the Kennel Club since 1953:

1953	..	8,129	1960	..	6,374
1954	..	7,356	1961	..	6,758
1955	..	7,275	1962	..	6,559
1956	..	7,071	1963	..	6,514
1957	..	6,434	1964	..	6,263
1958	..	6,515	1965	..	6,259
1959	..	6,943	1966	..	5,229

CHAPTER II

PAST HISTORY OF THE PARTICOLOURS

BETWEEN the years 1850 and 1860 Mr. Burdett owned a black and tan spaniel named Frank. He was mated to a black and white bitch called Venus, owned by Mr. Mousley. This mating produced a dog named Bob, which our great authority, Mr. H. S. Lloyd, states was the forerunner of the cocker spaniel as we know it on the show bench today. Most particoloured cockers as well as the blacks seem to have descended from the OBO strain. Mr. C. A. Phillips, of the Rivington cockers, owned many blue roans and black and whites, including Champions Rivington Dazzle and Rivington Robena. The late Mr. R. Lloyd bred a bitch Braeside Bizz which was mated to a black dog Viceroy. This pair appears to have possessed a lot of type, and the mating produced Braeside Bustle, who was one of the first dogs to transmit his blue roan colour regularly to his progeny. There are very few of the coloured cockers that cannot trace back to this outstanding sire, and there is little doubt that his progeny laid the foundation of many of our leading dogs of today.

Between the year 1900 and the First World War, many good particolour cockers were bred. Mr. De Courcy Peel, of the Bowdler strain, was well to the fore and owned a string of champions including Champion Ben Bowdler, who was sired by Braeside Bustle, also Champion Bob Bowdler, Champion Dixon Bowdler, and the great sire Champion Rufus Bowdler, who sprang into prominence at this time by siring three champions. Mr. E. C. Spencer's Doonys was another strain which helped the breed considerably. Doony Flirt was mated to Champion Ben Bowdler and this mating produced the blue roan Champion Doony Swell, who played a big part as a sire before the First World War. Mr. Gordon George's Fairholme Rally has been marked by the memorable success he scored as a sire, giving his offspring length of head which was so much needed in the early days. Rally was also a conspicuous field trial winner. Another great dog which had a remarkable influence at stud was Corncrake. His sire was Dyrons Bluecoat and his dam Rocklyn Betsy. Corncrake was himself a certificate winner in 1916 and was also the sire of many certificate winners. Between the two world wars we were rich in particolours; one of the first well-known dogs of that period was Champion Fulmer Ben, who won no fewer than twenty Challenge Certificates; he was owned by Mrs. Fytche. There was also Mr. Dickinson's Southernwood Critic, who as an inmate of the Rocklyn Kennel caused a sensation by winning the cup two years following at the Kennel Club Show for best dog of all breeds. Then we had Mr. Lloyd's Champion Invader of Ware, who was one of the greatest show and stud dogs of all time. Invader not only sired hundreds of winners but stamped his progeny with his great personality to a marked degree.

The Falconers strain owned by the late Mrs. Jamieson Higgens took a very prominent place in the show world and did a great amount towards bringing the particolour up to its present-day standard. Mrs. Jamieson Higgens was a great personality, whose passing left a grievous gap in the cocker world. Some of her best-known certificate winners were Falconers Chita, Spangle, Cowslip, Chance, Verdict, Clove, Caution, Confidence, and many others. The Falconers certificate winners followed one another without a break, all of which were home bred and had a definite individuality.

There was little breeding done between the years 1940 and 1945, when the war was in progress. Dog foods became very scarce, transport was difficult, and dog shows were few and far between; therefore many well-known kennels closed down during this period, but as soon as peace was declared everyone started breeding in a bigger way than ever before. To my mind the standard of the cocker today has improved considerably, and shows a marked advance on its predecessors of the show bench.

I think we can rightly say the two greatest cocker spaniel personalities of the post-war period are Tracey Witch of Ware, the blue roan bitch owned by Mr. H. S. Lloyd, and Oxshott Marxedes the light blue roan dog owned and bred by Mrs. Gold. Tracey Witch of Ware has created a post-war record by winning 50 Challenge Certificates, the first dog or bitch of any breed to

PEDIGREE OF THE B.O.B. CHALLENGE CHALLENGE WINNER SIR GALAHAD WARRANT ...

LIGHT BLUE ROAN. BORN 5-4-46 K.C.S.B. 1081 A.E.   JUNIOR WARRANT 123

Oxshott Marxedes

Sire: **FALCONERS MARK OF WARE**

- Falconers Workman of Ware
  - Sir Galahad of Ware (C.C.s)
    - Manxman of Ware (C.C.)
      - Whoopee of Ware
      - Devotion of Lewaigne
    - Falconers Confidence (C.C.s)
      - Silver Flare of Ware
      - Falconers Caution
  - Falconers Contest (C.C.s)
    - Whoopee of Ware (54 C.C.s)
      - Ch. Churchdene Invader
      - Foxham Minx
    - Falconers Carla
      - Dobrow Dash
      - Falconers Chita
- Falconers Wisdom
  - Sir Galahad of Ware (C.C.s)
    - Manxman of Ware (C.C.)
      - Whoopee of Ware
      - Devotion of Lewaigne
    - Falconers Confidence (C.C.s)
      - Silver Flare of Ware
      - Falconers Caution
  - Falconers Careful (C.C.s)
    - Silver Flare of Ware (C.C.)
      - Deebanks Marcus
      - Baxter Betty
    - Falconers Caution (C.C.)
      - Colnar Critic
      - Falconers Cowslip

Dam: **BERRAZANNE OF OXSHOTT**

- Oxshott Padgett
  - Falconers Padlock of Ware
    - Sir Galahad of Ware (C.C.s)
      - Manxman of Ware
      - Falconers Confidence
    - Falconers Careful (C.C.s)
      - Silver Flare of Ware
      - Falconers Caution
  - Red Rougette of Oxshott
    - Valclipse of Misbourne
      - Ch. Golfhill Eclipse
      - Valerie of Misbourne
    - Blaquette of Oxshott (J.W.)
      - Oxshott Barzanes
      - Bellona of Oxshott
- Lady Lancelot
  - Sir Galahad of Ware (C.C.s)
    - Manxman of Ware (C.C.)
      - Whoopee of Ware
      - Devotion of Lewaigne
    - Falconers Confidence (C.C.s)
      - Silver Flare of Ware
      - Falconers Caution
  - Blossomfield Butterfly
    - Ch. Foxham Migrant
      - Silver Flare of Ware
      - Cilrog Meg
    - Blossomfield Elizabeth
      - Dobrow Dash
      - Blossomfield Lady-in-Waiting

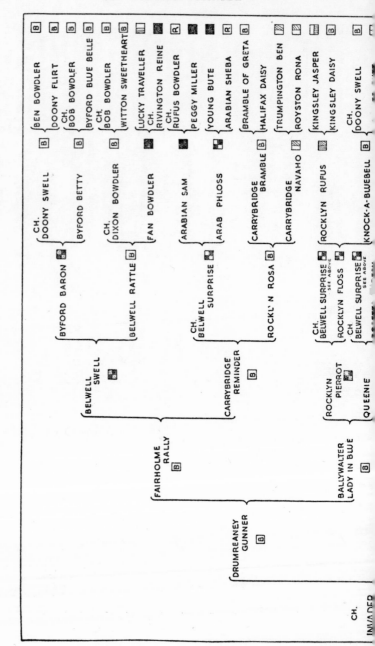

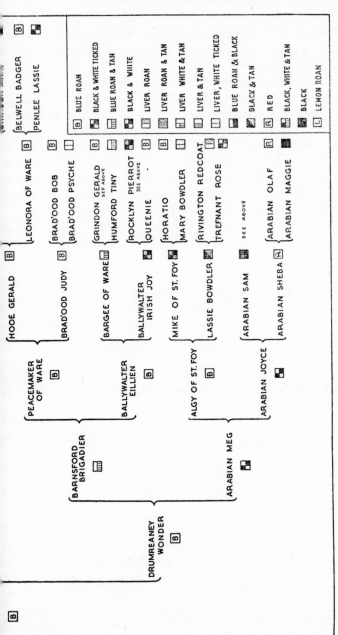

have achieved this. Born on May 10th, 1945, Witch is by Falconers Padlock of Ware out of a bitch named Whist. It seems Witch has every chance of beating the pre-war certificate record put up by Mr. Lloyd's beautiful black, white and tan bitch Exquisite Model of Ware, who won 53 Challenge Certificates and was also supreme champion of Cruft's on two occasions. Another celebrity from the same kennel was the blue roan dog Luckystar of Ware, who was supreme champion at Cruft's in 1930 and again in 1931. Whoopee of Ware gained 54 Challenge Certificates pre-war, believed to be a record for any breed of that time. Oxshott Marxedes has had 26 Challenge Certificates at the time of writing and has also had the distinction of winning two Challenge Certificates at Cruft's in the years 1948 and 1952.

I am not writing of any of the big winners of today in this Chapter, as I have referred to them in my list of certificate winners.

PEDIGREE OF CHAMPION INVADER OF WARE

Invader is acknowledged as one of the best blue roan dogs ever, and as a sire was unsurpassed. As a show dog he was exhibited in 88 classes and won 88 First prizes and 12 Challenge Certificates. He worked well in the field, and qualified for his title with flying colours—a dog which will always stand out in cocker history. *See* Pedigree on pages 24 and 25.

THE HISTORY OF THE RED COCKER

The late Mr. C. A. Phillips, who was President of the Cocker Spaniel Club, imported in 1896 from America a red cocker named Canadian Red Jacket, and a black cocker Toronto, who also had red breeding in his pedigree. A daughter of Red Jacket was mated to Toronto, producing a black bitch Latcho, and it was through this combination of American blood that Mr. and Mrs. Trinder under the prefixes "Arabian" and "Northwick" produced several red cockers. They were further assisted in establishing a red strain by the use of an imported black dog Hampton Guard, who was bred from a red sire and red dam. At the end of the 1914 war, Mr. E. E. Todd, who had been closely associated with Mr. Trinder for several years prior to 1914, continued the

"Arabian" strain using Arabian Red Jay for his post-war foundation. In the period of 1920–30 a number of breeders became seriously interested in the development of the red cocker and considerable assistance in the standardization of the colour was given by the late Mr. H. S. Lloyd's importation from Canada of the black cocker Broadcaster of Ware, an OBO descendant. His breeding cuts out about twenty-five years of English blood and goes directly back to the OBO strain. Broadcaster fully justified the wisdom of his importation by siring a big percentage of reds, and imparting supreme quality and type to his progeny, which helped considerably to popularize the red cocker.

Broadcaster was a direct descendant of the original OBO exported from this country to America, which I shall deal with in another Chapter. Another dog which did great things for the red cocker was Mr. H. S. Lloyd's imported American-bred Robinhurst of Ware. From this blood the majority of the reds of today have originated. The enthusiasm of the earlier breeders led to the formation, in May 1928, of the Red and Golden Cocker Spaniel Club with a membership of twenty-four. Mr. E. E. Todd was elected secretary, a post he has retained to the present day. Before the formation of the Club there was a fetish for the setter red colour, and it was not uncommon for the dogs of a lighter shade to be penalized at shows as "poor coloured". The title Red and Golden Cocker Spaniel Club overcame the prejudice against the golden specimens and there is little doubt that the varying shades did much to popularize the breed as a whole. Looking back over the years, one can appreciate the wisdom of the founders in accepting the standards laid down by the Cocker Club twenty-six years earlier, and confining themselves solely to the specialization of colours, with the result that the present-day reds and goldens can hold their own in any colour classes; today it is quite a common thing for a red to be awarded a certificate. The Club did much valuable work in guaranteeing separate colour classes at the principal open and championship shows, and up to 1929 provided red classes at Cruft's confined to members.

It is thought that mention should be made of the various prefixes which contributed to the development of the present-day reds and some relevant details are given in the following paragraphs.

The "Of Sauls" owned by Mrs. Southern. The principal

influencing red blood was obtained through Lady of Sauls, which was sired by the Canadian imported Broadcaster of Ware. Lady of Sauls mated to Herald of Ware produced Rufus of Sauls, who in turn sired Woodcock Ringleader and Billy of Byfleet, both of whom greatly contributed to the improvement of the reds.

The Lightwater prefix owned by Mrs. Pelham Sutton. This strain also had a big say in reds, and comprised a mixture of Pinbrook, Dyrons and Broadcaster blood.

The Padsons owned by Miss Stubberfield and Mrs. Spencer. This Kennel will be remembered by the black stud dog Joker of Padson, which was sired by Blackcock of Lightwater ex Youlden Firefly. Joker of Padson was the sire of the famous Bazel Otto, who also sired many reds.

The Byfleet strain was founded in 1926 by Mrs. M. K. Acton, who purchased two red bitches, Golden Emblem of Byfleet, who was sired by Pinbrook Bungy ex Sunshine of Lightwater, and Owlsmoor Pimpernel by Broadcaster of Ware ex Echo Busy Bee. Mating Golden Emblem to Ottershaw Lorenza she bred Benjamin of Byfleet and Ottershaw Bingo. Owlsmoor Pimpernel was mated to Bovington Red Lacquer and Delia of Byfleet. Brae of Brambletye and Ottershaw Pimpernel resulted from this mating. Mrs. Acton later mated Owlsmoor Pimpernel to Rufus of Sauls and bred Billy of Byfleet, who in turn was mated to a bitch Sporting Susan, who had Robinhurst of Ware blood on both sides. This produced Daffodil of Byfleet. It was then decided to try to make an improvement in the heads of the reds, so Daffodil was mated to the blue Luckystar of Ware, who possessed red blood coming through his grandfather Invader of Ware, Invader's grand-dam Arabian Meg being bred through two generations of Arabian Reds. Two reds, Stardust of Byfleet (winner of five Challenge Certificates) and Lodestar of Sorrelsun, resulted from the Luckystar and Daffodil mating. Lodestar of Sorrelsun was mated to Fay of Sorrelsun and produced Cleo of Byfleet, winner of three Challenge Certificates. Fay was by Woodcock Ringleader out of Benita of Byfleet, who was by Benjamin of Byfleet out of Delia of Byfleet. The offspring of the aforementioned dogs were interbred with occasional outcross matings to Woodcock Ebony, Waldiff Copper, and Treetops Talkie, and produced a large number of winners, including Deidre of Byfleet, Cara of Byfleet, Maro of Byfleet, Golden Glory of Byfleet, Jeanette and Beauty of Byfleet, Ottershaw Inego and Ottershaw Cedar, etc.

Sh. Ch. Sixshot Otto the Owl

Sh. Ch. Gatehampton Dumbo

F. W. Simms

Ch. Oxshott Marxedes

C. M. Cooke

Sh. Ch. Shooting Star of Hearts

The Dorswick cockers were founded in 1929 by Mrs. Wicks, who obtained from Mrs. Acton Jeanette of Byfleet ex Barbara of Byfleet and Golden Glory of Byfleet by Lodestar of Sorrelsun ex Deidre of Byfleet as her foundation stock. Jeanette of Byfleet mated to Treetops Tenor produced Treetops Tarentella, dam of Treetops Taurus and Treetops Tyrian, and from a mating to Treetops Trivet bred Alpheus of Dorswick and Frolic of Dorswick. Alpheus mated to Golden Glory of Byfleet bred Daylight of Dellcroft (dam of Treetops Torchbearer) and Armida of Dorswick, dam of Treetops Turkey Trot, one of the foundation bitches of the Lochranza strain. Alpheus was also the sire of Aingarth Daffodil, foundation bitch of the Aingarth strain. Frolic of Dorswick was the dam of Golden Miller of Dorswick, founder of the Donnett strain. Among other well-known dogs bred in the kennels were Brynful Barka, Treetops Tender, winner of three Challenge Certificates, Treetops Truculent and Treetops Traveller, C.A.C. winners, France; Sixshot Peggy Puffin, Germany, and Sixshot Sugar Bird, etc. Ten generations have been bred under the Dorswick prefix, and the breeding has been confined to dogs possessing the same blood-lines as the foundation dogs of the Byfleet strain. Mrs. Wicks had not been seen in the show ring for some years until she made a very successful "come back" in 1952 with her red dog Dorswick Golden Feather, who quickly won his junior warrant, a son of Sixshot Woodywoodpecker. Although the Dorswicks have not been shown they have continued to maintain their character and reputation.

Prefixes of some of the Red and Golden Breeders, 1922–39, who did so much towards the success and popularity that the red and golden cocker of today has achieved:

"Arabian"	Mr. E. E. Todd	"Ottershaw"	Mr. W. S. Hunt
"Beaunash"	Mrs. Cluckie	"Overdale"	Mr. J. G. Abell
"Bethersden"	Mrs. Adams	"Padson"	Miss Stubberfield
"Brambletye"	Mrs. R. Gow		and Mrs. Spencer
"Dellcroft"	Mrs. L. Childs	"Pinbrook"	Mr. W. H. Edwards
"Dorswick"	Mrs. Wicks	"Rivoli"	Mr. Bridgford
"Garnes"	Mr. A. G. Dickinson	"Rydals"	Mr. Oldfield
"Heydown"	Miss Carnegie	"Sorrelsun"	Mrs. Jourdain
"Lightwater"	Mrs. Pelham Sutton	"Walcott"	Miss A. S. Pryce
"Machars"	Miss Tory Edgar	"Waldiff"	Mrs. Shakespeare
"Merok"	Mr. and Mrs.	"Ware"	Mr. H. S. Lloyd
	McKinney	"Woodcock"	Mrs. McIntyre

SOME OF THE WELL-KNOWN RED CHALLENGE CERTIFICATE WINNERS, 1909–58

Name of Winner	Sire	Dam
Fairholme Kathleen	Rivington Regent	Galtress Nell
Pinbrook Amber	Pinbrook Colin	Pinbrook Peggy
Stardust of Byfleet	Luckystar of Ware	Daffodil of Byfleet
Nene Valley Sanfoin	Woodcock Ringleader	Nene Valley Sunflower
Cleo of Byfleet	Lodestar of Sorrelsun	Fay of Sorrelsun
Horseshoe Primula	Woodcock Ringleader	Ottershaw Pimpernel
Woodcock Polly	Woodcock Ringleader	Woodcock Prima Donna
Flamengo of Glenbervie	Ottershaw Perseus	Ottershaw Myrna
Treetops Turtle Dove	Treetops Terrific	Sixshot Mavis (later Treetops Temptress)
Stocks Honeysuckle	Jester of Laurel	Lady Burlesque
Treetops Tristan	Bazel Otto	Treetops True Love
Lymas Crookrise Fortune	Bramlyn Bartlemy	Carol of Cravensdale
Treetops Truce	Treetops Tyrian	Treetops Tendril
Broomleaf Bonny Lad of Shillwater	Blare of Broomleaf	Caroline of Shillwater
Craigomus Critic of Ide	Golden Rule of Ide	Crocus of Aingarth
Golden Rule of Ide	Ch. Golden Rod of Ide	Ringlands Pin-up Girl
Lochranza Lisbon Story	Treetops Truce	Lochranza Laughing Imp
Glenbervie Chieftain of Two Pools	Sandcote Golden Falcon	Catcote Commotion
Treetops Tender	Treetops Tenant	Mimosa of Dorswick
Treetops Tailormaid	Treetops Foxbar Cognac	Treetops Red Tulip
Golden Rod of Ide	Sixshot Black Swan	Lotusflower of Sorrelsun
Golden Star of Ulwell	Sixshot Willy Wagtail	Romance of Ulwell
Golden Valerie of Durban	Sixshot Willy Wagtail	Maison Belle
Knoleforth Dyrad	Sixshot Willy Wagtail	Cherry of Bridene
Broomleaf Primula of Kenavon	Sixshot Willy Wagtail	Kenavon's Bran of Broomleaf
Sh. Ch. Sixshot Woodywoodpecker	Sixshot Willy Wagtail	Sixshot Nightingale
Bonny Lass of Kenavon	Ch. Broomleaf Bonny Lad of Shillwater	Bramble of Kenavon
Sunkist Lotus Lily	Golden Rule of Ide	Crocus of Aingarth
Broomleaf Ballet Shoes	Broomleaf Kim of Churdles	Brown Bess of Broomleaf
Gatehampton Dumbo	Broomleaf Ernocroft Event	Gatehampton Sunrise
Cassa Chance	Sh. Ch. Sixshot Woodywoodpecker	Roscott Susie
Golden Wagson of Ulwell	Sh. Ch. Golden Star of Ulwell	Olican Caramel of Ulwell

Name of Winner	*Sire*	*Dam*
Sh. Ch. Sixshot Storm Bird	Sixshot Woodywoodpecker	Sixshot Cuckoo
Broomleaf Camelia of Dorswick	Sixshot Woodywoodpecker	Honeysuckle of Dorswick
Broomleaf Black-eyed Susan	Billy Budd of Broomleaf	Bubbley of Broomleaf
Lochranza Eldwythe Elegance	Lochranza London Tan	Solinda of Traquair
Sh. Ch. Sixshot Shore Lark	Sixshot Storm Bird	Sixshot Moor Hen
Bazel Sovereign	Dunford King	Bazel Oonah

PEDIGREE OF WOODCOCK RINGLEADER

Ringleader had a very great influence at stud and helped considerably in bringing the reds up to the present-day standard. He was the sire of many famous winners, a very beautiful dog and could no doubt hold his own in the show ring today with our up-to-date reds. (*See* Pedigree on page 32.)

PEDIGREE OF LODESTAR OF SORRELSUN

Lodestar of Sorrelsun was litter sister to Champion Stardust of Byfleet, and sire of many famous winners, including Cleo of Byfleet, who won three Challenge Certificates. (*See* Pedigree on page 33.)

SOME OF THE NOTED BLACKS

Dominorum D'Arcy, although fifty per cent colour bred, sired only three particolours, all of which were Certificate winners, namely, Dame Fortune of Ware, Apex of Ware, and Charleston Lyric.

There is little doubt that D'Arcy was the key to the present-day blacks. His daughter Dunford Judy mated to Joker of Padson produced the great Bazel Otto. Otto was mated to Felbrigg Hortensia and the litter resulting produced Treetops Treasure Trove, the foundation of the Treetops cockers. In turn Treasure Trove was mated to Woodcock Ringleader and this mating produced Treetops Talkie and Treetops Trivet. Treetops Talkie mated to Treetops Treasury produced Treetops Terrific. Sixshot Mavis was also mated to Bazel Otto. This mating

Pedigree of Woodcock Ringleader

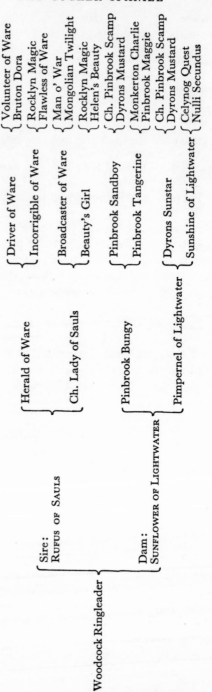

Woodcock Ringleader

Sire: RUFUS OF SAULS

- Herald of Ware
  - Driver of Ware
    - Volunteer of Ware
    - Bruton Dora
  - Incorrigible of Ware
    - Rocklyn Magic
    - Flawless of Ware
- Ch. Lady of Sauls
  - Broadcaster of Ware
    - Man o' War
    - Mongolian Twilight
  - Beauty's Girl
    - Rocklyn Magic
    - Helen's Beauty

Dam: SUNFLOWER OF LIGHTWATER

- Pinbrook Bungy
  - Pinbrook Sandboy
    - Ch. Pinbrook Scamp
    - Dyrons Mustard
  - Pinbrook Tangerine
    - Monkerton Charlie
    - Pinbrook Maggie
- Pimpernel of Lightwater
  - Dyrons Sunstar
    - Ch. Pinbrook Scamp
    - Dyrons Mustard
  - Sunshine of Lightwater
    - Celynog Quest
    - Nulli Secundus

PEDIGREE OF LODESTAR OF SORRELSUN

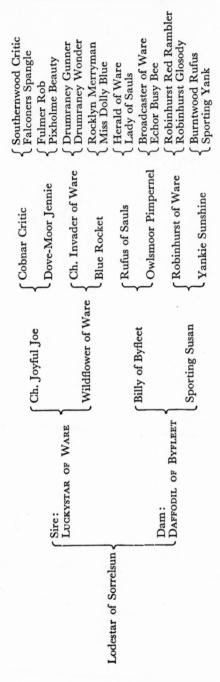

Lodestar of Sorrelsun

Sire:
LUCKYSTAR OF WARE

Ch. Joyful Joe
- Cobnar Critic
  - Southernwood Critic
  - Falconers Spangle
- Dove-Moor Jennie
  - Fulmer Rob
  - Pixholme Beauty

Wildflower of Ware
- Ch. Invader of Ware
  - Drumraney Gunner
  - Drumraney Wonder
- Blue Rocket
  - Rocklyn Merryman
  - Miss Dolly Blue

Dam:
DAFFODIL OF BYFFLEET

Billy of Byfleet
- Rufus of Sauls
  - Herald of Ware
  - Lady of Sauls
- Owlsmoor Pimpernel
  - Broadcaster of Ware
  - Echor Busy Bee

Sporting Susan
- Robinhurst of Ware
  - Robinhurst Red Rambler
  - Robinhurst Glosody
- Yankie Sunshine
  - Burntwood Rufus
  - Sporting Yank

Pedigree of Dominorum D'Arcy

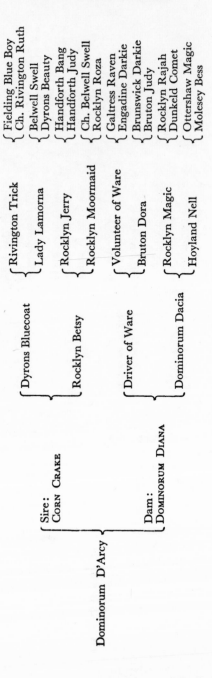

Dominorum D'Arcy

Sire: CORN CRAKE
- Dyrons Bluecoat
  - Rivington Trick
    - Fielding Blue Boy
    - Ch. Rivington Ruth
  - Lady Lamorna
    - Belwell Swell
    - Dyrons Beauty
- Rocklyn Betsy
  - Rocklyn Jerry
    - Handforth Bang
    - Handforth Judy
  - Rocklyn Moormaid
    - Ch. Belwell Swell
    - Rocklyn Roza

Dam: DOMINORUM DIANA
- Driver of Ware
  - Volunteer of Ware
    - Galtress Raven
    - Engadine Darkie
  - Bruton Dora
    - Brunswick Darkie
    - Bruton Judy
- Dominorum Dacia
  - Rocklyn Magic
    - Rocklyn Rajah
    - Dunkeld Comet
  - Hoyland Nell
    - Ottershaw Magic
    - Molesey Bess

PEDIGREE OF SIXSHOT BLACK SWAN

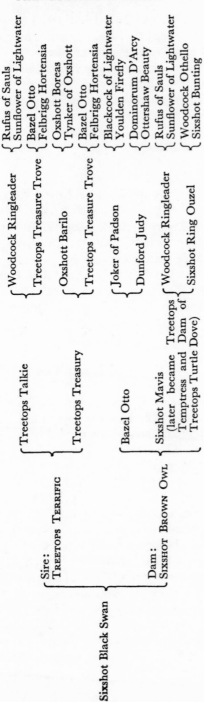

Sixshot Black Swan

Sire: TREETOPS TERRIFIC

- Treetops Talkie
  - Woodcock Ringleader
    - Rufus of Sauls
    - Sunflower of Lightwater
  - Treetops Treasure Trove
    - Bazel Otto
    - Felbrigg Hortensia
- Treetops Treasury
  - Oxshott Barilo
    - Oxshott Boreas
    - Tynker of Oxshott
  - Treetops Treasure Trove
    - Bazel Otto
    - Felbrigg Hortensia

Dam: SIXSHOT BROWN OWL

- Bazel Otto
  - Joker of Padson
    - Blackcock of Lightwater
    - Youlden Firefly
  - Dunford Judy
    - Dominorum D'Arcy
    - Ottershaw Beauty
- Sixshot Mavis (later became Treetops Temptress and Dam of Treetops Turtle Dove)
  - Woodcock Ringleader
    - Rufus of Sauls
    - Sunflower of Lightwater
  - Sixshot Ring Ouzel
    - Woodcock Othello
    - Sixshot Bunting

produced Sixshot Brown Owl, who, when mated to Treetops Terrific, produced Sixshot Black Swan. The above dogs had practically all the say in the pre-war blacks.

It may interest readers to study the pedigrees of Dominorum D'Arcy and Sixshot Black Swan. (*See* Pedigrees on pages 34 and 35.) During the war breeding was very much curtailed and blacks suffered considerably until in 1956 Sixshot the Black Cockatoo was placed at stud and through this dog the blacks are of a higher standard than ever before.

PEDIGREE OF SIXSHOT BLACK SWAN

Sixshot Black Swan, I think I can rightly say, was one of the best black dogs ever. His brilliant show career was cut short by the outbreak of war. He came from a line of very famous bitches, and made a great name as a stud dog. Figuring in most of the whole colour pedigrees of today, he was home-bred, and owned by me until his death in 1951, at the age of twelve and a half years. (*See* Pedigree on page 35.)

THE BLACK AND TAN

The original colour of the cocker spaniel was either black and tan or liver and tan. In those early days blacks were rare, and it was considered a great achievement when a whole litter of blacks were bred. The late Mr. R. Lloyd, father of Mr. H. S. Lloyd, owned a black and tan dog named Little Prince, who was, incidentally, the sire of the first champion owned by the "Of Ware" Kennels, although in those days the suffix "Of Ware" had not been adopted. For many years the black and tan lost favour with the exhibitor, and very few were seen at the shows, until Mrs. Doxford brought out the bitch which was aptly named Broomleaf Black and Tan, a daughter of Champion Broomleaf Bonny Lad of Shillwater, out of the blue roan and tan Butterfly of Broomleaf. From her first appearance in the ring, Black and Tan became the subject of much criticism and caused quite a sensation, when she won her first Challenge Certificate at the Richmond Championship Show in 1949. At the time of the Show Black and Tan was already in whelp to Oxshott Pendarcye, a mating which was expected to produce a black and tan, as Pendarcye carries coloured blood. The litter resulted in six all blacks, which at the time was somewhat disappointing. However, one of the black dogs was retained and named Black Friar of Broomleaf. It was felt he would undoubtedly sire some puppies of his dam's colour, but, alas, his first four bitches failed to produce a black and tan; his fifth bitch was a red by Eros of Padson, and from this mating two black and tans turned up, which was a great joy. His next bitch was Blanchfleur of Broomleaf, a daughter of Blare of Broomleaf. She also produced two of this elusive colour; one dog was retained and named Brainwave of Broomleaf, who did so well at Cruft's in 1952, competing against all colours. The day is not far distant when we shall see many of this fascinating colour in the show ring. I feel that to see this colour at its best, they should be in a class of their own. Who knows? In years to come they perhaps will become as popular as the reds, who have made such great headway in recent years.

THE STANDARD AND ITS USES

The standard of the cocker laid down by the Kennel Club is indispensable, as it indicates to the beginner what points to breed

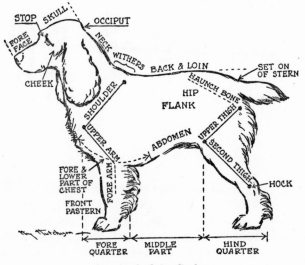

Standard of the Cocker

for, but the best education for the novice is to attend Championship Shows, where one can see good dogs in the flesh and study the points of each one individually. The novice breeder may have a small kennel of useless specimens, but perhaps one very much

Bad head   Good head

better than the others. He becomes impressed with this one dog, the pick of a poor bunch, and if he never sees a better elevates him into a standard. So many novice breeders never see beyond the head, but a good head alone will do little towards gaining top

Bad front: narrow   Bad front: bowed   Good front

honours in the show ring. The novice will do well closely to study the points, and if your dog fails badly in one of them he will not go very high in the prize list. Much money and precious time will have been wasted in travelling the country to the various shows. When the novice is making a start in building up his stock he must have in mind the type he aims at. Among show dogs of today there is a wide diversity of type, which is an advantage. Therefore you can win with a cocker providing it complies with the standard, although it retains a marked individuality of your own individual strain. You can often sit at the ringside and pick out the progeny of a well-known stud dog, as some have the happy knack of stamping their own particular attributes; it is a great advantage, if the said dog is the type desired. There are different types within the limits of the standard. We get the masculine short cobby type and the feminine racy type; a dog which has type is not always perfect, but embodies much of the ideal cocker. Type is most difficult to define; you have only to look at the interpretation of the standard as seen by different judges and if you follow their placings you will see one favours

Good hindquarters   Bad hindquarters

the short cobby masculine cocker, whereas another will go for the feminine racy one. All this will no doubt appear very complicated to the novice, but if he makes a study of judging it will soon become clear.

THE STANDARD POINTS OF THE COCKER SPANIEL

The following is the standard of points approved by the Kennel Club, and reproduced with their kind permission, dated January 1950.

General Appearance.—That of an active, merry, sporting dog. The Cocker Spaniel does not follow in the lines of the larger Field

Spaniel, either in lengthiness, lowness or otherwise, but is shorter in back, and rather higher on the legs.

Head and Skull.—A nicely developed square muzzle and level jaw; with distinct stop. Skull and forehead should be well developed, with plenty of room for brain power, cleanly chiselled and not cheeky. Nose sufficiently wide and well developed to ensure the exquisite scenting power of this breed.

Eyes.—Full but not prominent, hazel or brown coloured, harmonizing with colour of coat, with a general expression of intelligence and gentleness, decidedly wide-awake, bright and merry.

Ears.—Lobular, set on low, leather-fine and not extending

Bad tail placement

beyond the nose; well clothed with long silky hair, which should be straight; no positive curls or ringlets.

Neck.—Should be long and muscular, and neatly set on to fine sloping shoulders.

Forequarters.—The shoulders should be sloping and fine, chest deep and well developed, but not too wide and round to interfere with the free action of the forelegs. The legs must be well boned, feathered and straight, and should be sufficiently short for concentrated power, but not too short to interfere with the tremendous exertions expected from this grand little sporting dog.

Body.—Compact and firmly knit together, giving the impression of a concentration of power and untiring activity. Short in back. Immensely strong and compact in proportion to the size and weight of the dog; slightly drooping towards the tail.

Hindquarters.—Wide, well rounded and very muscular. The

legs must be well boned, feathered and straight and should be sufficiently short for concentrated power but not too short to interfere with its full activity.

Feet.—Should be firm, round and cat-like, not too large or spreading or loose-jointed.

Tail.—This is characteristic of blue blood in all the varieties of the Spaniel family. In the lighter and more active Cocker, although set low down, can be allowed a slightly higher carriage

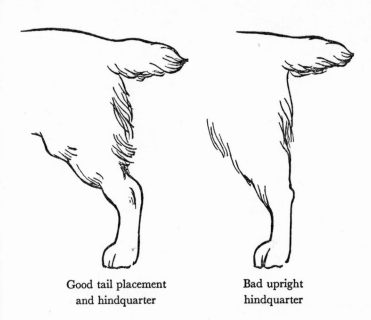

| Good tail placement and hindquarter | Bad upright hindquarter |

than in the other varieties, never cocked up over, but rather in a line with the back; the lower the carriage the better; when at work its action should be incessant in this the brightest and merriest of the whole Spaniel Family. Not docked too short.

Coat.—Flat and silky in texture, never wiry or wavy, with sufficient feather; but not too profuse, and never curly.

Colour.—Various; in self colours no white is allowed except on the chest.

Weight and Size.—The weight should be about 25 lb. to 28 lb.

Faults.—Coarse skull, light bone, curly coat, straight shoulders, feet, poor movement, weak hocks, high tail carriage, deficient stop, light eyes.

Scale of Points for Judging Cocker Spaniels

Positive Points

Head and Jaws	10
Eyes	5
Ears	5
Neck	10
Body	20
Fore-legs	10
Hind-legs	10
Feet	10
Stern	10
Coat and Feather	10
Total Positive Points	100

Total Negative Points

Light eyes	10
Light nose	15
Hair curled on ears (very undesirable) . .	15
Coat (curly, woolly, or wiry) . . .	20
Carriage of stern	20
Top Knot	20
Total Negative Points	100

The Of Wares

As I have previously mentioned in the history of the cocker, the Of Wares were established as far back as 1875 by the late Mr. R. Lloyd, father of the late Mr. H. S. Lloyd. We cocker enthusiasts have a great deal to thank both father and son for; they have certainly played a tremendous part in bringing the cocker up to its present-day standard. Having very scanty material to work with, they brought order out of chaos, thus laying the foundation and enabling we other cocker breeders to carry on. Many winners were bred in the Of Ware Kennels in the early days, which have helped considerably in building up contemporary history; a very large number of cockers throughout the world have been the progeny of the Of Ware stud dogs. They have also had the honour of being six times supreme champion of Cruft's, the greatest show in the world. The kennel is now carried on by Miss Jennifer Lloyd, the third generation of Lloyds.

FALCONERS

The Falconers Kennel owned by the late Mrs. Jamieson Higgens was never a large one, and taking this into account it must be regarded as the most consistently successful of all. The strain produced a string of notable bitches, which took a prominent place in the show world.

LOCHNELL

Mrs. Cameron is a breeder of many years standing and must be given an honourable place in the cocker world. Dozens of famous specimens have been bred by her, which are winning not only in England, but throughout the world. The latest star is Sh. Ch. Val of Lochnell.

TREETOPS

The Treetops Kennel owned by Mrs. de Casembroot was established in 1932, founded on the beautiful black bitch Treetops Treasure Trove.

Tremendous strides to the front were made in a very short time. As a show bitch Treasure Trove had a great run of success, and climbed to Challenge Certificate status. As a brood bitch she became equally famous, and her name can be traced back in most of the whole colour winning pedigrees of today. When mated to Woodcock Ringleader she produced Treetops Talkie, who quickly brought the prefix to the fore. As a stud dog Talkie was in great demand and sired countless winners, his progeny developing a definite individuality. Yet another good brood was Treetops Treasury, dam of the famous Treetops Terrific, one of the greatest black sires of all times. I always had a tender spot for Terrific as he was the sire of my own Sixshot Black Swan. Treetops Foxbar Cognac is another very important black sire. In the red section Treetops Tristan, Tenor, Tyrian, Truce, and Tennant have had a great influence on the reds.

BROOMLEAF

The Broomleafs have consistently been in the forefront at most of the championship shows in recent years. Mrs. Doxford's brilliant purchase of Champion Broomleaf Bonny Lad of Shillwater has indeed repaid her in full; he quickly became a champion after joining the Broomleaf Kennel. For this his owner deserves full marks, as he was trained for his title entirely by her. Bonny Lad is a son of Blare of Broomleaf.

To name only a few of the bitches that reside at Broomleaf, I mention Ballet Shoes, Primula, Delia, Black and Tan, Black-eyed Susan, Boots and Shoes and Bonffante, all of which are Show Champions. Latest star is the lovely black dog, Sh. Ch. Blackbird of Broomleaf.

COLINWOOD

Mr. A. W. Collins has owned several champions, specializing in the attractive black white and tan. Of the many good dogs housed at the Colinwood Kennels I should say Cowboy takes first place, and has done much towards bringing the Colinwoods into the prominent position they hold today. He has also played a big part in helping to maintain the breed's high standard; all his progeny carry his distinction and character. To name just a few of the important dogs at Colinwood, I mention Son-of-a-Gun, Roughrider, Cossack, Howitzer and the fabulous Silver Lariot, one of the most famous ever of any breed. Mr. Collins has now handed the kennel over to his daughter, Miss P. M. Collins.

GATEHAMPTON

Among the pillars of the modern breeders must be included Mrs. Cloke of the Gatehampton cockers who has had a great run of success with home-bred stock. Many good ones have been benched from this select Kennel. Gatehampton Buttercup, who did a considerable amount of winning, produced Gatehampton Farmers Lad and Gatehampton Farmers Lass. It would be difficult to mention all the famous winners from this Kennel, but the four most important are the certificate winners, Gatehampton Dumbo, Gatehampton Jennifer, Gatehampton Billy Boy, Sh. Ch. Gatehampton Black Sambo of Lochnell and Gatehampton Golden Tango of Leadhill.

Sh. Ch. Dellah Merry Maker of Wykey

Ch. Luklena Musical Maid

Head Study of Sh. Ch. Sixshot Woodywoodpecker

Innharmony Chorister

MISBOURNE

The Misbourne Kennel owned by Miss Dorothy Hahn was established many years before the war. Specializing chiefly in blacks which are exhibited all over the country with a considerable amount of success. The most famous being Pickpocket of Misbourne, Sh. Ch. Wendayle Valjolie of Misbourne, Sh. Ch. Valjoker of Misbourne, and Sh. Ch. Atways My Love of Misbourne.

KENAVON

The Kenavon cockers are housed at Shepperton, Middlesex, and are owned by Miss Betty Mingay, who quickly established a reputation for breeding high-class stock, attaining remarkable success with a string of red bitches. All are bred on intelligent, scientific lines and have made their mark on the breed. Some of the best-known are Bonny Lass of Kenavon, Broomleaf Primula of Kenavon, Glenbervie Wisdom of Kenavon, Pelynt Wistful of Kenavon, Patterns Primrose of Kenavon, Broomleaf Delia of Kenavon, Kenavon's Delight, and the red dogs Bonny Lad of Kenavon, Broomleaf Maestro of Kenavon, Happy Fella of Kenavon, and Sh. Ch. Crackshill Alpine Crocus.

WEIRDENE

The Weirdene Cockers are housed in Scotland and since the war have gone full steam ahead, their enthusiastic owner is to be seen at most of the championship shows throughout the British Isles, many Weirdene champions have left these shores, but new faces quickly replace them, as this book goes to print, Sh. Ch. Wells Fargo of Weirdene and Sh. Ch. Woodlark of Weirdene are at the head of affairs.

NOSTREBOR

The Nostrebor Kennel is a small, select one and has been in the forefront at most of the important shows in recent years. The blue roan dog Nostrebor Chayn Weaver is a well-known sire and has done a lot towards helping to maintain the prestige of the blues. Other well-known dogs in this Kennel are Nostrebor

D

Marco of Hy-Niall, a certificate winner, also the young blue dog Nostrebor Eldwythe Excellency and Nostrebor Nickel Coin is an outstanding red. Nostrebor Neapolitan is the latest certificate winner.

LOCHRANZA

The Lochranza cockers owned by Miss Macmillan were founded in the inter-war period. One of the foundation bitches, Treetops Turkey Trot, produced many winners, and from her offspring a definite strain soon developed. Stock of high quality has been bred. The male Champion Lochranza Latchkey won his title in keen competition, a black dog of immense personality. Another to have made a name for this Kennel is the beautiful red bitch Lochranza Lisbon Story, who secured several certificates. There are many other famous winners, the latest being Sh. Ch. Lochranza Dancing Master Sh. Ch. Lochranza Merryleaf Eigar, and Lochranza Darnclever.

IDE

The Of Ide Kennel, owned by Mr. Joe Braddon, is a long-established one. It was originally in Devon but afterwards moved to the Stratford-on-Avon district. The Of Ides are exhibited all over the country with a good share of top honours, and I think I am right in saying that at the present time there are more full champions owned by this Kennel than any other. As a show dog and sire Champion Golden Rod of Ide has been one of the most renowned and has deservedly made his full title. The beautiful tricolour bitch Champion Rodwood Lass of Sandover has piled up many enviable wins, including best of all breeds in show at the Leeds Championship, 1952. There are many other famous dogs, the latest star being the black and white dog Domino of Ide.

THE OF HEARTS

The Of Hearts cockers are famous throughout the world, owned by Mr. Hubert Arthur of Llanelly, South Wales, pride of place should be given to the two champion brothers Shooting Star of Hearts and Silver Mogul of Hearts, a powerful kennel of high class stock.

CHAPTER III

BREEDING

IF there were any underlying principles which definitely produced winners, dog breeding would become simple indeed—too simple. It would lose its joy and fascination, and also its value. Everyone would be breeding winners, therefore winning dogs would become two a penny. Needless to say this is not the case, even nowadays when we have so many good stud dogs to choose from. If one succeeds in breeding a "top notcher", by this I mean a certificate winner, it is a great achievement. There are probably hundreds of winners bred yearly but so few good enough to go on winning when they are out of the junior classes, although breeders of past years have accomplished wonders in the development of the modern cocker. There are certain principles founded on the experience of modern breeders which are well worth studying. Most breeders who have the love of the cocker at heart are only too pleased to give a word of advice to the novice, which should help him to make a right start. As I shall mention later in this Chapter, your fundamental stock is most important. Always seek information about the faults of the ancestors of your brood bitch when you are choosing your stud dog; avoid using a dog with any of these faults. If you study pedigrees you can soon form a fairly clear idea as to how the famous dogs of today were produced. In blacks Dominorum D'Arcy played a big part, as did Bazel Otto, Treetops Talkie, Treetops Terrific, Sixshot Black Swan and of the present-day Treetops Foxbar Cognac has done his share, and Champion Lochranza Latchkey. Turning to the reds we have Rufus of Sauls and his son Woodcock Ringleader, who figure in most of the red pedigrees. Robinhurst of Ware, imported from America by Mr. H. S. Lloyd, did a lot to improve the reds in his day. Then we have the Byfleets and Lodestar of Sorrelsun, who was by the blue Luckystar of Ware. Champion Golden Rod of Ide has bred many winners, so has Blare of Broomleaf and his illustrious son, Champion Broomleaf

47

Bonny Lad of Shillwater, also Sixshot Willy Wagtail and his son Sixshot Woodywoodpecker.

In particolours we have the great Invader of Ware, who probably did more for his colour than any dog in history. Falconers Mark of Ware was the sire of Champion Oxshott Marxedes and Champion Rodworth Lass of Sandover. The famous Tracey Witch of Ware was by Falconers Padlock of Ware. From Sir Galahad of Ware through the Blackmoors came that outstanding sire, Champion Colinwood Cowboy.

It may be of interest to study the pedigrees of some of our famous sires. They will be found in this book.

BREEDING AS A HOBBY

If you intend to start a cocker Kennel as a hobby and run it successfully it should just about pay its way, with perhaps a bit on the right side, providing all goes well and you have no setbacks. The first thing is to obtain your stock, so you can make a start, and for this be sure to go to a reliable breeder. A couple of really well-bred bitches should be sufficient to start with, if it is pet puppies you intend to breed. When the time comes, mate to a reasonably good dog, and try to sell your puppies at the age of eight to ten weeks, or as soon as they are ready to go; the longer you keep them the less profit you will get—you might even find yourself out of pocket. Never be persuaded into buying a stud dog as, unless you are a well-known exhibitor, it will cost you far more in advertisements than you will see back in stud fees. If you mean to go in for show stock a different start should be made, and the importance in selecting a good brood bitch cannot be overstressed. A great number of novice breeders, intending to take up dog breeding, have a mistaken idea that any sort of bitch mated to a famous stud dog will produce a champion. I have so often heard, "She is not a good specimen, but I intend to mate her to a good dog and get something to show and win with." If their belief is put into practice they will no doubt be heading for disaster; in my opinion it is equally important to select a first-rate brood bitch as it is a good stud dog, and if one is lucky enough to find a brood bitch which can turn out consistent winners she is worth her weight in gold. It is the secret of successful dog breeding.

Presuming you have your puppies, and they are now eight weeks old, perhaps you could get some experienced person to advise you which to keep. Do not attempt to run on too many, in the hope that they will all turn out winners, as your Kennel will soon get filled with fully grown nondescript cockers, which will be difficult to find homes for, unless you are prepared to let them go for a few pounds, and they will have already cost you very much more to bring up. Therefore your bank balance will suffer. I find that when people are buying a pet they prefer a puppy under six months, and are usually willing to pay much more for it at that age. It is a mistaken idea to suppose you will get more for them when they are grown up, unless of course you have a show specimen, which is quite a different proposition. A few promising puppies may be run on for four or five months, when your experienced friends will probably again review them for you. There are many disappointments in dog breeding, and you may find that after all your puppies are not up to show standard and will have to be sold as pets. But do not despair. In your next litter you may breed the very puppy you have been dreaming of, and you will be well rewarded for all your previous troubles and disappointments.

Nevertheless, the beginner with little practical knowledge and no comprehension of dogs must not expect to make a lot of money for several years after he has started his Kennel. He cannot hope to compete with breeders who have spent a lifetime at it, so I should say that providing your dogs are showing a small profit and have not become a drain on your pocket you are on the road to success.

INBREEDING AND LINE BREEDING

The relationship of ancestors is an important factor in dog breeding, plainly due to the consideration that related animals are more alike than unrelated ones. Therefore the nearer alike two parents are, the greater is the possibility that their children will possess most of their good points. The aim is to breed a cocker with all the good qualities of the parents, and if possible to make an improvement. If inbreeding is resorted to, which is the mating of stock closely related, such as sire and daughter, dam and son, or brother and sister, both dogs should be free from any physical defect. Mental soundness is of the greatest importance and can be bred for as much as any physical feature. Do not attempt to breed from a nervous bitch, however beautiful she may be; the temptation will be great, but it is not worth the risk. The nervous trait is almost certain to come out, if not in the first generation it will crop up again later, and you will finish up by having a Kennel full of nervous cockers. If they are to be shown, dog-showing will become a nightmare to you and your dogs. Most experienced breeders favour line breeding, and if you study the pedigrees of the majority of famous winners you will find they have been bred this way. Line breeding is the mating of less closely related stock than inbreeding. To line-breed successfully one should have a thorough knowledge of the breed. For instance, supposing a strain does not excel in heads and a mating is being contemplated with a dog who has a good head, his ancestors for three generations back should be considered to see if they have any failing in this feature. Throwing back and unwanted faults can crop up when least expected. Consequently the pedigree on both sides should be studied and the family characteristics gone into. You cannot go on inbreeding or line breeding for too long, as you are likely to produce nervous, highly strung cockers. When you have established your strain you will need to bring in an outcross—which means the mating of unrelated stock. This is extremely valuable in breeding out some weakness that may have crept in, or to correct some fault which is becoming prevalent, probably the result of inbreeding for too long. So many breeders are inclined to neglect the female side and will breed from a bitch so much below standard. So the breeding of a good cocker becomes more difficult; the dams' influence will be quite equal to that of the sires'; to mate a poor quality bitch to a first-rate dog is no reason why the progeny should inherit all the good points of the stud dog. Some of them may, but they are also just as likely to inherit the bad points of the dam. Faults are much more easily transmitted than are the good qualities; therefore too much attention cannot be paid to the defects of your breeding stock if you wish to make headway in the show ring.

As an illustration, let us imagine we are founding a strain. As we have said before, a strain is something that is established; we must inbreed as a means to the end. Strain may be termed an element, not only so far as physical attributes are concerned but one also able to transmit characteristics with some degree of regularity. Should heads be the prime consideration in our supposed strain, other points should not be subjugated; but if your breeding stock fails to reach the first objective you must not breed from them again. Naturally it should be determined whether or not the point we seek appears strongly enough in the pedigree. Mathematically we have one half, one quarter, and one eighth, going back through the pedigree. This divided in half expresses the possibilities of both sire and dam, so far as prepotency is concerned. If the individuals have been selected to the same standard each controls fifty per cent of the offspring, backed by these individual ancestors: sire to daughter gives us seventy-five per cent of the sire's blood—a daughter from this mating bred back to the original sire gives us eighty-seven and a half per cent of the sire's blood in the offspring. Son to mother produces the same resultant fraction, giving the preponderance in the dam's blood. Mating the offspring back to the original stock will show where the prepotency of each character lies. If a son mated to his mother sires puppies resembling her, her prepotency is established, although the young son may resemble his father. The same applies to the mating of father and daughter. By mating a dog with three-quarters of his father's blood to a bitch with the same amount of her mother's blood we should produce puppies resembling to a large degree the original pair. By continuing with these matings we produce a family of unvarying type. Thus we are breeding by the law of mathematics.

Inbreeding without discrimination will spell disaster. The novice should be well acquainted with his subject before attempting to inbreed. Then we have the outcross, a matter of supreme delicacy. Some lines of blood suit other lines of blood; there are others that will not mix in at all satisfactorily, so one must first take into consideration blood lines of the past, and if a certain outcross suited a certain bloodline years ago it is possible that a similar outcross will suit it again today. If you wish to make a success of breeding, all this is well worth studying. I have seen dire results from outcrossing when the blood lines have not suited, but as I have said earlier you cannot go on inbreeding for too long; you must bring in an outcross occasionally, as inbreeding may retain and accentuate the show type but in the end deterioration of the breed is certain to come.

The Stud Dog and the Visiting Bitch

It is unwise for the novice breeder to commence with a stud dog. Wait until you are well known in the show ring before attempting to place a dog at public stud. Advertising is very expensive and the dog will not make enough to pay his bills. A successful stud dog must come from a line of good bitches, so you should become established in your bitch line before attempting to breed a dog for stud. The bitch line behind him is of the greatest importance, therefore his dam, also her ancestors, will have a great influence on the quality of the puppies he will sire. Past history of the breed will prove this, so if you have to take your bitch to another breeder to be mated choose a suitable stud dog, and if possible choose one largely on the merits and breeding of his dam. To become a successful breeder you must look further than the dog—although the sire plays a very important part you cannot expect him to do it all. It is no use flying off to the latest sensational sire with a poor sort of bitch expecting to breed a champion. Your aim should be to keep improving your stock, but it will need endless patience; it cannot be done in a hurry. Make a point of getting good foundation stock. If you make a wrong start your progress will be slow; it is better to start with one good bitch than half a dozen poor specimens. You sometimes hear of a beginner breeding a champion in his first litter, but usually if you probe into this you will find he started with a good bitch. The better your bitches, the higher the grade of puppies you will breed, and the greater your chances are of breeding a first prize winner. The stud dog must be in perfect health and condition. He will need to be fed liberally, with good raw beef, eggs, milk, or any of the vitality-giving foods, but should never be allowed to get over-fat. He will also need plenty of good, regular exercise. A popular stud dog is always very sought after, but owners who study the welfare of their dog will strictly limit the number of bitches they allow to visit him. If a stud dog is well looked after and not overworked he will go on for many years, siring big, strong litters, but if a dog is overdone when he is young he will be useless after a few years. So if you have a dog and you value him it will pay you in the long run not to overtax his strength by having too many bitches.

If you have no stud dog of your own when you contemplate

breeding from your bitch you will find there are many good dogs advertised at stud to choose from, and when you have finally made up your mind get in touch with the owner of the stud dog and book a service. Immediately the bitch to be bred from is in season, notify the owner of the stud dog so that he will be able to reserve him for you. It will be to your own advantage to send word at once, then the dog will be kept for you and other bookings will not be accepted.

If the bitch is to be sent by rail, use a roomy travelling-box with plenty of ventilation. Do not despatch her until the ninth day of her season. That will be quite soon enough. She may be your dearest little pet but the owner of the stud dog will not want to keep her longer than is necessary, as she will have to be locked up very securely in a kennel alone, which she will no doubt object to. She will probably bark day and night, which will not be good for her, nor will it be for the nerves of anyone within hearing. Always remember to pay return carriage your end; this will save the owner of the stud dog a lot of trouble. When sending your bitch by rail for a long distance it is better to send by night, when she will probably sleep through the journey. Before despatching, enquiries should be made as to the route by which she will travel and the time of arrival at her destination, in order that the person to whom she is being sent can be on the look-out for her. It is advisable for the sender to instruct the recipient to wire or telephone should your bitch fail to arrive at the given time.

I find the railways very considerate on the whole with all livestock, and do their utmost to see they arrive at their destination as soon as they can.

The best type of travelling-box is one with a peaked roof; it is not possible to pile luggage on a box of this sort, therefore it is not likely to be overlooked. Also, see that there are plenty of air-holes, although during hot weather this will not be sufficient— part of the woodwork should be removed and replaced with either chain link netting or iron bars. Painted on the box in bold letters should be "Valuable live dog". A strongly made travelling-box such as the one described is a most useful and necessary adjunct to a Kennel; apart from sending a dog away by rail, it is a most convenient way of taking a dog in a car to a show, compelling it to stay in one place and not be at liberty to jump from one seat to another, which is such a danger to the driver. Also, if you have an ill dog which is in need of constant attention night and day, and it is more convenient to have it indoors, a box of this sort will be most useful as an indoor kennel. It must be remembered that a travelling-box should be of such a height that the dog can stand upright without any difficulty.

All stud fees are payable in advance, or at the time of mating. Most owners allow a return service, if the bitch should not prove in whelp to the first mating, but it is not legally enforceable as the fee paid is for the service given, with no guarantee that a litter will result from the mating. If a return service is given, the owner of the stud is within his rights to insist that the second service be to the same bitch at the next season. The payer of the stud fee has a right to be present at the serving of his bitch, if he wishes.

When you mate a young dog for the first time start if possible with an experienced brood bitch. You should not attempt to use him before the age of ten months, and if he does not appear keen wait for another month before trying again. Do not force him. Some dogs are later maturing in this way than others. From the start let him know the bitch will be held for him. This will give him confidence; so many bitches will snap at a dog when being mated and this is inclined to put some young dogs off, particularly if they get badly bitten.

The dog will become locked or tied to the bitch during mating, so that he cannot get free for approximately ten to thirty minutes, or even longer. Without this tie fertilization is very doubtful, although on rare occasions you hear of puppies being born when there has been no tie. Once the mating is accomplished it must be remembered to keep a strict eye on your bitch for a week or so as she will probably be very eager to accept further attentions from any dog that might come her way. During this period the chosen dog can repeat the mating, if you think it advisable, although there is no necessity for two matings if the first one is satisfactory. When the dog has mated the bitch, and the tie is effected, the bitch should be held by the collar, so that she is unable to drag the dog about and perhaps injure him by causing a rupture.

When can you tell if your bitch is in whelp? It is difficult to say with certainty; some show earlier than others, but you should know five weeks after the mating has taken place. One of the first indications of conception is that the bitch may eat indifferently; on the other hand, she may become very hungry, or perhaps vomit her food and become lazy. At the sixth week there is usually a round of the flanks; at this stage the bitch should be fed three times daily instead of the one big meal. I shall deal with this matter in another Chapter.

The Brood Bitch

If you are hoping to breed puppies of sufficiently high standard to enter the show ring the importance of the choice of your brood bitch cannot be overstressed. Only the best is good enough if you aim to breed show stock. It is quite impossible for us all to be in a position to pay a big price for a show bitch, so the next best thing is to get one with no glaring fault, of superb breeding. Most of the well-known breeders are able to supply a bitch of this sort. The bitch line counts for so much; she must be equally well bred on both sire and dam sides. Her immediate forebears should be good; do not rely on dogs two or three generations back to produce your winners—if you do you will no doubt be disappointed. It does happen sometimes, but the chance is almost negligible. If you are successful in finding a bitch fulfilling all the requirements of the perfect brood she will be of untold value and should never be parted with.

It is wise not to mate your bitch until the second heat, unless of course she does not come into season until twelve months of age, which is often the case. It is a mistake to mate a bitch too young; a litter will be developing and born before she herself has finished growing. This would be a great strain on her, although many are of the opinion that a bitch in the wild state would breed as soon as nature permitted. This may be so, but dogs have become domesticated and are very different from the dogs of long ago, when they were in their wild, natural state.

Having settled on your brood bitch, now is the time to find your stud dog. Use a dog which is producing winners. There are many famous stud dogs available. In making your choice remember that the bitch line behind him is of great importance. Do not use a dog whose female ancestry is unknown; he may be a chance bred one and will make a very poor sire. Then your puppies would be suitable only for the pet market, and valuable time would have been wasted. Do not choose a stud dog of an entirely different type from your bitch. You will get better results from a dog of similar appearance, providing he is good enough.

CELIBACY

Celibacy is unnatural. It is good for all bitches to have at least one litter in their lives, and—who knows?—after you have had the pleasure of breeding one litter you may become a regular breeder. Many famous exhibitors have begun this way.

THE BITCH IN SEASON

Sexual behaviour is seasonable in most animals, but when a bitch reaches the age of about eight months (and in certain cases younger or later) oestrum will occur; in other words, the bitch will be "in season". The condition is recognized by the swelling of the organs. At first there will be a clear mucous discharge, followed by a red discharge which usually continues for ten or twelve days. In some cases it will clear up earlier, in others it will go on longer. This is followed by a heavy white discharge which will go on for another few days. In normal cases the heat lasts from three to four weeks. During the "in season" period a bitch will change her habits considerably: she will become very skittish, always out for a game, and perhaps she may become faddy with her food. Generally speaking, however, you should watch for your bitch puppy coming in season at about the age of eight months, although it may not occur until the age of ten or twelve months or even later—I have known bitches not to come in until eighteen months of age. In very rare instances a bitch does not come in season at all; in a case of this sort you should see your veterinary surgeon.

Another very trying thing for a breeder: a bitch will sometimes have what is called a false heat, coming in season long before she is due. This condition is difficult to recognize from a true heat. The bitch will even stand to be mated, but does not prove in whelp, and just when she is due for her puppies she will come in season again. This time she may be mated with every success. Often bitches will show colour for a week or even longer after mating—it may be they have been mated too early. If it does not continue for too long it may be disregarded.

After its first appearance the heat should recur about every six months, but there again you cannot always be certain to a

TABLE SHOWING WHEN A BITCH IS DUE TO WHELP

Served January.	Due to Whelp March.	Served February.	Due to Whelp April.	Served March.	Due to Whelp May.	Served April.	Due to Whelp June.	Served May.	Due to Whelp July.	Served June.	Due to Whelp August.	Served July.	Due to Whelp September.	Served August.	Due to Whelp October.	Served September.	Due to Whelp November.	Served October.	Due to Whelp December.	Served November.	Due to Whelp January.	Served December.	Due to Whelp February.
1	5	1	5	1	3	1	3	1	3	1	3	1	2	1	3	1	3	1	3	1	3	1	2
2	6	2	6	2	4	2	4	2	4	2	4	2	3	2	4	2	4	2	4	2	4	2	3
3	7	3	7	3	5	3	5	3	5	3	5	3	4	3	5	3	5	3	5	3	5	3	4
4	8	4	8	4	6	4	6	4	6	4	6	4	5	4	6	4	6	4	6	4	6	4	5
5	9	5	9	5	7	5	7	5	7	5	7	5	6	5	7	5	7	5	7	5	7	5	6
6	10	6	10	6	8	6	8	6	8	6	8	6	7	6	8	6	8	6	8	6	8	6	7
7	11	7	11	7	9	7	9	7	9	7	9	7	8	7	9	7	9	7	9	7	9	7	8
8	12	8	12	8	10	8	10	8	10	8	10	8	9	8	10	8	10	8	10	8	10	8	9
9	13	9	13	9	11	9	11	9	11	9	11	9	10	9	11	9	11	9	11	9	11	9	10
10	14	10	14	10	12	10	12	10	12	10	12	10	11	10	12	10	12	10	12	10	12	10	11
11	15	11	15	11	13	11	13	11	13	11	13	11	12	11	13	11	13	11	13	11	13	11	12
12	16	12	16	12	14	12	14	12	14	12	14	12	13	12	14	12	14	12	14	12	14	12	13
13	17	13	17	13	15	13	15	13	15	13	15	13	14	13	15	13	15	13	15	13	15	13	14
14	18	14	18	14	16	14	16	14	16	14	16	14	15	14	16	14	16	14	16	14	16	14	15
15	19	15	19	15	17	15	17	15	17	15	17	15	16	15	17	15	17	15	17	15	17	15	16
16	20	16	20	16	18	16	18	16	18	16	18	16	17	16	18	16	18	16	18	16	18	16	17
17	21	17	21	17	19	17	19	17	19	17	19	17	18	17	19	17	19	17	19	17	19	17	18
18	22	18	22	18	20	18	20	18	20	18	20	18	19	18	20	18	20	18	20	18	20	18	19
19	23	19	23	19	21	19	21	19	21	19	21	19	20	19	21	19	21	19	21	19	21	19	20
20	24	20	24	20	22	20	22	20	22	20	22	20	21	20	22	20	22	20	22	20	22	20	21
21	25	21	25	21	23	21	23	21	23	21	23	21	22	21	23	21	23	21	23	21	23	21	22
22	26	22	26	22	24	22	24	22	24	22	24	22	23	22	24	22	24	22	24	22	24	22	23
23	27	23	27	23	25	23	25	23	25	23	25	23	24	23	25	23	25	23	25	23	25	23	24
24	28	24	28	24	26	24	26	24	26	24	26	24	25	24	26	24	26	24	26	24	26	24	25
25	29	25	29	25	27	25	27	25	27	25	27	25	26	25	27	25	27	25	27	25	27	25	26
26	30	26	30	26	28	26	28	26	28	26	28	26	27	26	28	26	28	26	28	26	28	26	27
27	31	27	May 1	27	29	27	29	27	29	27	29	27	28	27	29	27	29	27	29	27	29	27	28
28	Apr. 1	28	2	28	30	28	30	28	30	28	30	28	29	28	30	28	30	28	30	28	30	28	Mar. 1
29	2	29	3	29	31	29	July 1	29	31	29	Sep. 1	29	30	29	31	29	Dec. 1	29	31	29	Feb. 1	29	2
30	3			30	June 1	30	2	30	Aug. 1	30	2	30	Oct. 1	30	Nov. 1	30	2	30	Jan. 1	30	2	30	3
31	4			31	2			31	2			31	2	31	2			31	2			31	4

month or so. When the bitch has been mated it often recurs when her puppies are four months old, or six months after the previous heat. Until all signs of season have completely disappeared the bitch must be most carefully protected or she is almost certain to get out and mate herself, to perhaps an uncertain character she will not mind if he is a champion cocker or the lowest scruffy mongrel. Some bitches will go to any extreme in order to get out and travel for miles followed by a retinue of dogs, whilst others are quite indifferent about the whole thing.

The greatest menace of all are the crossbred street dogs. They will scent and trail a bitch for miles; therefore never let her off the lead when being exercised. It is surprising how a dog can suddenly appear from nowhere, even in the midst of the country when you think it is quite safe to let your bitch have a lovely scamper over the moors. If your bitch has been mated, and her season is over, let her have as much natural freedom as possible right up to the time she is due to whelp. Both she and her puppies will be all the better for it. Failure to take care of one's bitch when in season, and failure to control a dog when there is obviously a bitch about in that condition, is one of the worst forms of neglect.

The Bitch in Whelp

A bitch in whelp should have every care and attention. The success of her litter will depend largely on the way she has been looked after during pregnancy. She will need plenty of nourishing food, although it is imperative to avoid excessive fatness as this is likely to cause difficulty at whelping time. You cannot do better than to give her a liberal supply of raw beef, or horseflesh; about three-quarters of a pound to a pound daily should be sufficient. This could be divided, and given with some rusked brown bread or biscuit morning and evening. In addition, an egg beaten with milk is good, and a teaspoonful of cod liver oil. Also, calcium can be added to her meal. Some favour the more sloppy foods for the bitch in whelp, but I have found the above diet very satisfactory. A good teaspoonful of milk of magnesia every morning will be very beneficial, as, apart from being a mild laxative, it will reduce the risk of acid milk, which causes the death of so many puppies.

A bitch will need exercise right up to the last, or as long as he can take it without discomfort, but do not overdo her. If you are conveniently situated, let her have as much natural freedom as possible.

Bitches in whelp should be free from worms, particularly because they may be passed on to the unborn puppies through the blood-stream. It is wise to worm her a fortnight after mating if you see any signs of worms.

The bitch should be given a box for whelping in, large enough for her to stretch herself out. It is wise to have a ledge all round the inside, about two and a half inches wide and three inches from the floor. This will prevent the bitch crushing the puppies on the side of the box, and many lives will be saved this way if your bitch is clumsy. It is wise to prepare the bed where she is to have her puppies some time before. If you move her just as she is due to whelp you will be asking for trouble. Do not attempt it; she will probably not settle and as the puppies are born she will try to carry them back to her old bed and you may lose the lot in consequence. Whatever bedding you put into the box before whelping will possibly be scratched out, so it is best to give very little of any kind. Avoid a loose blanket or anything of that sort; it will more likely than not get bunched up and suffocate the puppies. I find the most successful way to make a bed in the box is to put a thick layer of hay in the bottom and then tack a piece of sacking over this; it can be easily removed for washing, and it will help the puppies when they are sucking as they seem to get more of a grip with their paws than if they are in a box with a plain wood surface.

The full period of gestation is sixty-three days from the time of mating, although it is a common thing for the puppies to be born a few days early; but there is no need for worry, within the limits of a few days or so, before or after. If the puppies are born six days too soon they very seldom survive. Some bitches go one or two days over the normal time, but providing your bitch is fit and well and not straining there is little you can do about it. Should she begin straining and no puppy is born after a couple of hours, send for your veterinary surgeon as in such circumstances something might be wrong. One can usually tell within a few hours when a bitch is going to whelp. There is a disinclination for food and possibly the last meal she has eaten will be vomited; she will seek a quiet spot if she is not already alone in her kennel, and will probably pant, start to scratch and make a bed. Her temperature will probably drop as low as 98 degrees. Cockers in general are easy whelpers and no difficulties should be expected. The puppies are usually born at night and in the normal way there should be no need to sit with her after the first puppy is born, but you cannot make a hard and fast rule about this as bitches vary. Some become rather highly strung and your presence will give them confidence, particularly if they are house pets, but the normal bitch will much prefer to be quite alone, and anything disturbing her will upset the procedure of a natural whelping. The owner should let two hours go by, then have a glance to see that all is well. The bitch is usually capable of doing everything for herself, but if she fails to sever the cords of the puppies it is advisable to tie a thread ligature tightly round the navel cords, about an inch from the puppies' bodies, and sever the cords with scissors sterilized before use. After the first puppy is born the bitch may be offered a little warm milk, and if she seems at all exhausted a few drops of brandy may be added. Often the last puppy in the litter is born some time after the others, the bitch being busy attending to her little family at this stage, not continually straining. There will be no need for worry. When the litter is born the bitch should be left to settle down quietly. She will not need much in the way of food for the first day or so, apart from plain milk or a little Bengers food made with milk may be offered. There is normally a raised temperature for the first couple of days, hence the liquid diet; also, it must be remembered that each puppy born is followed by an after-birth, a dark, nasty, greenish-looking mass which is eaten by the bitch. It is quite right and proper for her to consume it, therefore do not interfere with her at all. This is nature's way of providing nourishment for the exhausted mother. Do not disturb her by cleaning out her bed immediately after the whelping—a little job of this sort can wait until the mother has had a well-earned sleep. After some hours she will come out to relieve herself, then you can clean up her box and also sponge her down with a weak solution of disinfectant, drying her well, and if she is a good mother she will be very eager to get back to her family. Do not worry the bitch by frequently visiting her kennel; she will herself do all that is necessary for the puppies.

After the first few days she will need plenty of good food, and to be let out of her kennel for short outings, two or three times daily. It is wise to leave the pups untouched for the first twenty-

The Of Wares

Cavalier   Mark   Marcus of Akron   Countess Chloe   Tracey Witch   Hyperion

Sh. Ch. Broomleaf Black and Tan

Ch. Craigleith Cinderella

four hours; this will be time enough to discover their sexes, although one is always so curious, and no matter how many litters one has bred there is always the thrill: maybe in this litter there will be a certificate winner.

The first milk given by the bitch is called colostrum and its composition gradually changes until it becomes milk proper. The colostrum is a mild laxative, and one of its purposes is to eliminate the impurities which will possibly have accumulated in the puppies during the period of gestation. It is reasonable to assume that the change in the composition of the milk would be completed within about twenty-four hours.

The feeding of the puppies can be left entirely to the mother for the first three weeks after whelping. Puppies are very easily fatally chilled if they stay away from their mother and are unable to find their way back, so if they are born in the cold winter months heating may be necessary, such as a lamp or an oil stove in the kennel; it will depend upon the amount of care given by the mother. If an oil stove is used great care should be taken to place it in a position where it cannot be knocked over. A healthy cocker should not need heat, unless the weather is exceptionally cold.

Perhaps it is hardly necessary to warn the owner, or whoever might be in charge, not to allow visitors or another dog to approach the mother and her young family for several weeks. If she is a good mother she will resent this and may become very excited, which in turn will have a detrimental action on the milk, and the puppies will suffer in consequence.

FALSE PREGNANCY

A false pregnancy is not an uncommon thing. It is more likely to occur in nervous, hysterical bitches which, after being properly mated, though not in whelp, assume an appearance of pregnancy and behave in every way as if they were going to have a litter. When the time is due for the puppies to arrive nothing but a little discharge comes away, and the bitch gradually gets back to her normal size. There will be milk; if a large amount some if it will need removing but not in sufficient quantity to leave the glands empty, otherwise the flow is stimulated. The treatment for the condition is the administration of Sex Hormone,

E

which can be supplied only by your veterinary surgeon. Maiden bitches with strong leanings towards maternity are also known to have a false pregnancy during the weeks following a season, apart from any question of mating. They will also develop a secretion of milk in the glands, and the abdomen will become enlarged and give a general picture of pregnancy. This is an effort of nature in accordance with what should have taken place had the bitch been mated and was to have a litter. In a case of this sort it is not advisable to leave her in one of your rooms alone, between the seventh and ninth week, as she is liable to tear up cushions and scratch all the stuffing out of chairs, but if you are unlucky enough to experience this do not be too hard on the bitch, she is just trying to make a bed—it is nature's way, not destructiveness.

THE FOSTER-MOTHER

One seldom loses a bitch when she is giving birth to her puppies, but should such an unfortunate thing happen one has to decide whether to put the puppies down or bring them up by hand. You may be lucky enough to get a foster-mother. There are one or two Kennels who hire bitches out for this purpose—you will often see them advertised in the dog papers—or perhaps your local vet can help you. He may know of a bitch with an unwanted litter, and the owner might be pleased for the bitch to bring up your puppies, particularly if you gave one in return for her services. You must be quite certain that the bitch used as a foster-mother is perfectly healthy, has a good supply of milk and is not bad-tempered. Also, her time of whelping should be more or less the same day as that of the bitch whose puppies she is to rear. The composition of a bitch's milk changes daily, and will be too strong for the newly-born puppies unless the time of whelping of the two bitches was about the same time. Before introducing the puppies to the foster-mother they should be well rubbed over with the foster-mother's milk; if she licks them and allows them to suck, you know all is well.

To bring puppies up by hand is a thankless job, and needs a lot of thinking about. They will need to be kept warm and constantly fed, which means getting up two or three times during the night. And after all your work you may lose them. However, if you decide to take on the task you will need a fountainpen filler and, later, a small feeding bottle. Start the first day with glucose and water at blood heat, and continue with one of the puppy foods mixed according to directions. If you can keep them going until the age of three weeks they should be all right, as at that age they will begin to lap; also, you may give them a tiny morsel of scraped lean beef. I once reared a litter by hand, but I never wish to take the job on again; it was the most tiring thing I had ever undertaken.

DOCKING

Most books will tell you to dock your puppies' tails at about three days old, but I have had better results in docking at six days. At this age they are stronger and more able to face any setbacks. The operation must be performed with docking scissors or a pair of sharp scissors well sterilized before use. A little more than half the tail should be removed. After the operation the area should be freely dabbed with iodine. The bleeding as a rule soon ceases and the healing can be left to the mother, although it is wise to be watchful for a few days.

At the same time as the docking of the tails the dew-claws should be removed. They are small semi-circular nails which grow on the inside of the front legs just above the feet and very occasionally on the hind legs. It is wise to remove them as, apart from looking neater when the dog grows older, they often grow round into the leg, causing considerable pain; or, if working in the field, they will probably get torn when going through thick cover or bramble. Rounded operating scissors are best for removing them, or a pair of curved nail scissors are equally successful. It is kinder to take the mother right away whilst the operation is in progress. If correctly done, very little pain is caused as at this age the tail is only cartilage, and you will find the puppies feeding from the mother immediately she is put back to them, a few minutes after the operation.

If you are quite a novice, and have had no experience of docking and removing dew-claws, it would be as well to get your veterinary surgeon or an experienced breeder to dock your first litter. You will then see how it is done, and should be able to do your following litters without any help.

WEANING

As I have said previously, until the age of three weeks the puppies can be left to the dam, assuming she has a good supply of milk and is liberally fed. During the first few days after whelping the bitch should be fed on milky foods, such as groats made with milk, an egg beaten up, or any of the patent milk foods. On the third day steamed fish may be given. If all is well with the mother, and she is nursing a big litter, you will find her very hungry so she should be fed four times a day. After the fourth day the bitch can go back to her normal diet, and should be given raw beef, well boiled tripe, fish, eggs, brown bread, etc. All the time she is feeding her pups she will need extra food. Changes in food can be made; she will also need milk foods, porridge made with milk, Slippery Elm food, and any of the innumerable milk foods available are very helpful in stimulating lactation.

The eyes of the puppies should open between the ninth and eleventh days, and at this stage the puppies will be crawling about, although they have not their full power of vision until about three weeks.

At the age of four weeks weaning is usually commenced. The first indication you get of this is that the bitch will vomit her partly digested food for her puppies to eat. This is a natural thing and should not be interfered with; it is nature's way of providing the pups with half-digested food until they are at an age when they can digest their own. I have heard of several novice breeders thinking there was something wrong and sending for their veterinary surgeons post haste. You must be careful at this stage not to allow the mother large pieces of meat. I once had a puppy choked in this way, so immediately I know weaning is in progress I feed the dam on foods that cannot harm the puppies when vomited. If the bitch brings up too much of her food to the puppies it is wise to keep her away from them for a couple of hours after she has had her meal; it will give her time to absorb some for herself, otherwise she will get into a very low state—you could give her a little extra food at this time.

Now is the time to give the puppies their first lesson in lapping. Most puppies will take milk at blood heat, slightly sweetened with either glucose or sugar. Begin by dipping their noses once or twice into the dish—a very shallow one is needed when they are so young. Goats' milk is excellent but for town dwellers somewhat difficult to obtain. Arrowroot or any of the baby foods are very useful. It is wise to feed the puppies separately, then you know each one has had his share, as some eat more quickly than others. Starting with two meals a day of about a dessert-spoonful at each meal, increase during the following week to three meals a day, and so on until at the age of seven weeks they are getting five meals daily. At this age a dessert-spoonful of raw minced meat can be added to their diet. Five meals a day sounds rather a lot, but it is better to feed little and often as puppies' digestion becomes so quickly upset.

About five weeks after birth the mother should be allowed to leave the puppies for a few hours daily. It is now time they got used to being without her. I find a very good thing is to provide a bench or a low platform where the dam can get away from the too persistent attentions of her little family, as by this time their teeth and claws are sharp.

Usually the dam has ceased to secrete milk when the puppies reach the age of eight weeks and the weaning is complete. The mother having done her duty to her family, it is now in the hands of the breeder to take over. When puppies reach the age of three months you can start cutting their meals down and at the age of four months three meals daily should be sufficient, providing the meals given have adequate nourishment.

In regard to the various foods for a growing puppy, give plenty of good raw meat, milk, boiled fish and rice. A hard biscuit, or a big bone with the bits of lean meat left on, will be very helpful to their teeth. Cod liver oil is very good for them; a teaspoonful can be put in one meal a day. Although they will need plenty of good food never overload them, or you will upset their digestion. Great care must be paid to the cleanliness of food bowls or dishes, and freshness of food is most important. On no account should left-over food be given the next day, particularly soaked dog biscuit, which becomes sour if not used almost at once. At seven to nine months puppies in most cases are fully grown, but they are not fully developed until twelve to eighteen months, sometimes even later than that. According to the law, they cease to be puppies at the age of six months and then require dog licences, but according to the Kennel Club they are puppies up to the age of twelve months and can be shown in puppy classes until that time, but they cannot be shown except in litter classes under the age of six months. If shown as a litter they must be over six weeks and not more than three months of age. There is considerable risk in showing puppies so young; therefore it is wise not to allow anyone to handle them—possibly some kind admirer may have stroked and patted a hundred dogs before arriving at your bench and is liable to pass on a germ which might mean losing your whole litter.

A few more remarks may be appropriate here. You cannot be too particular about the cleanliness of the bedding and of the puppies themselves. Start to groom at an early age with a soft brush. As mentioned earlier, always see that the feeding utensils are scrupulously clean. Puppies will not thrive amid dirt. Also see that they are free from insects, especially lice, as they cause great discomfort, and if heavily infested the puppy will soon become in poor condition. I do not believe in frequently dosing with medicine, a procedure to which some dogs seem to be subjected by their owners. If puppies are thoroughly and efficiently wormed during puppyhood, and thereafter are properly fed with good nourishing wholesome food and exercised regularly, they should ordinarily require no medicine.

CHAPTER IV

Feeding. Grooming. Elizabethan collar. Exercise. Trimming. Bathing. Housing. Purchasing a puppy. Selling a puppy. Training the house pet. The novice exhibitor. Training for the show ring. After the show. Nervousness in show dogs. An intelligent dog. Essentials for the novice to remember.

FEEDING

A DOG's natural food is raw meat, and this should be treated as the most important item in his diet. The dog by nature is carnivorous, or meat-eating, and in his wild state hunts and kills his own food, pulls it apart and devours it. The gastric juices in a dog's stomach are very strong and are capable of dissolving almost anything, including bones. Possessed as he is of these strong digestive powers he should be allowed to use them. Although dogs will eat farinaceous or starchy foods, they are not sufficient to keep the dog in good health and hard condition. If biscuit meal is given as a full meal I recommend that it is scalded first with a good stock made from bones. Apart from the addition providing extra nourishment, hound meal or such-like swell with moisture; therefore, if a dog is given a large quantity it will expand in his inside and give him bad indigestion. Presuming all cockers are like my own, he would wolf it down without stopping to think of the consequences. A healthy cocker is by nature greedy—in other words, he loves his food.

Adult dogs should be given two meals daily, the principal one consisting of either raw or lightly cooked meat, and the small one of good dog biscuit. There are dozens of different kinds to be had, so it is wise to give a change as dogs like variety in food the same as human beings do. Also, a daily drink of milk is very good for all dogs, and almost essential for puppies. I usually give my dogs a large raw bone to gnaw once a day after their big meal; apart from assisting dentition, it promotes the flow of saliva, which in turn helps to digest the food. As to the quantity of food to be given, it is difficult to make a hard and fast rule. Some dogs need more than others; also, stud dogs and bitches in whelp will need to be liberally fed. Normally a cocker should have a good half pound of raw meat daily, exclusive of his biscuit meal. If you find your dog getting too fat, decrease the biscuit meal but not the meat; lean meat is not fattening and will help to keep him in condition. With a large Kennel of dogs the food bill must be kept down if you are to make your dogs pay their way. You must get good nourishing food as cheaply as possible. Bullocks' heads are a good investment, but they will want really well boiling, until the meat falls off the bones. If you then cut up the meat and drop it back into the boilings with a little rice or oatmeal, and perhaps a few carrots, boil together until thoroughly cooked, then leave until the following day, you will find the whole mixture will turn out in a solid jelly which you can cut up in squares, and the dogs will love it. Every bit can be used this way; it is most economical, apart from being nutritious. It is surprising the big amount of meat you will find on a bullock's head.

If you want to put an extra bit of weight on your dog, herrings are excellent for this; if very well boiled they can be mashed up, bones and all, and brown bread or hound meal added to soak up the boilings. This will quickly put body on your dog if given alternate days, and if he is a good doer. I find dogs appreciate a bit of good cooking.

Paunches are another useful thing to add to the Kennel larder. They should be cheap, are very nourishing and the dogs love them. They also need well boiling. I always give a meal of paunch to a visiting bitch on arrival, if we have it, and I have never known one to leave it, a fact which speaks for itself.

If you cannot get cow beef, horse flesh is very good but unless bought as fit for human consumption it is wise to cook it thoroughly before use; it might have come from an animal which died of disease and would upset your dog's inside. Never feed frozen meat—it should always be allowed to thaw out before use—as this will also upset your dog. Rabbits are very good for tempting the appetite of a sick dog, care being taken to give no bones. The same applies to game or poultry bones; these can be very dangerous because if bitten up and swallowed they are liable to splinter and perforate the intestines.

Do not overfeed your dog. A healthy dog will clear up all that is given to him and ask for more, but be firm and give him just his ration. Do not give him all the tit-bits from the dinner table; collect the scraps and make one dish of them by adding broken biscuit or brown bread and good gravy. The ultimate result of overfeeding will ruin his health and his figure; he will become a fat, lazy dog, spending his life eating and sleeping. Too much sloppy food upsets a dog's inside, and deprives his digestive organs of their exercise.

The important part played by vitamins in a well-balanced diet is a comparatively recent discovery, yet judging by what dogs eat they appear to have always known that foods rich in vitamins were essential for their well-being. In the springtime it is quite a common thing to see dogs rush for the fresh green grass, which is so rich in vitamins; they can also get vitamin D through the action of the sun on their coats. Anyone who has kept a dog will have noticed how impatient he is to be out in the spring sun after the dark days of winter. When dogs lick themselves it is not only for toilet purposes—they are transferring the vitamin crop which has accumulated in their coats.

Some dogs like all kinds of fruit and it is really very good for them, an obvious fact when you stop to consider the proportion of essential vitamins it contains. Apples appear to stimulate the digestion and keep the teeth clean and wholesome. When they are plentiful it is a good idea to give your dog an apple to play with instead of a ball.

GROOMING

Every dog should be well groomed daily. Apart from stimulating and cleansing the coat and skin it will keep him free from parasites such as fleas and lice—a well-groomed dog seldom gets infested with these pests. It also keeps him free of odours and dandruff and will remove dead hair. The brush is the symbol of canine hygiene so use it regularly. Use it not once a week but every day if only for a few minutes; it will work wonders with your dog's appearance. Use vigorous motion, brush all parts, and do not forget to brush gently the ears inside and out and the leg featherings. I like the dandy best, the same sort that is used on horses but smaller. Start at the head and work downwards to the tail.

Then comes combing. There are numerous different types of combs; the best to use for a cocker is the steel No 6. You will find this very useful for the body coat and with the help of the brush it will remove most of the unwanted hair. You will need to use the comb very sparingly on the ears; it might thin out the ear featherings too much if used drastically. Finally, finish off with a chamois leather or hand glove; if this is done daily the coat will be in lovely bloom. Special attention should be paid to the inside of the ears. If they are cleaned out regularly with a piece of cotton wool, and a little boracic powder dropped in, they seldom give trouble.

The majority of dogs look forward to their daily brush. I find my own cockers each morning after they have had their breakfast lined up waiting to be groomed, and they become quite impatient until their turn comes to be lifted on to the table.

How often should dogs be bathed? Most people wash dogs too frequently; an occasional bath is all that is necessary. It requires a week for a dog to get the natural oil back into his coat. The daily brushing will do as much good as a bath. In the summer months ticks are often picked up by dogs living in the country and coming in contact with sheep, or playing on ground where sheep have been grazing. They will sometimes become infested with these revolting insects. They are greyish in colour and about the size of a small pea. You usually first notice them when they have feasted themselves with blood and their bodies are to be seen standing away from the skin. They generally attack the head and ears. They fix themselves firmly in with suckers and the only way to remove them is to place a little paraffin or methylated spirits on the insects which will sometimes cause them to release their grip. Leave on for several minutes before attempting to pull out, taking great care not to break off the head as if left behind it will cause a sore. After removal it is wise to apply a little antiseptic ointment to the affected area.

Another insect to beware of is the Harvest Bug, found at harvest time as their name denotes. This is a small red insect, looking like sand. It usually attacks a dog on the head and legs but can quickly be got rid of by any of the parasite powders.

The greatest menace of all in the summertime is the common grass seed. This is contacted on any waste ground or common land throughout this island. By mid-July the stalks have ripened and become brittle; then the seed heads can easily break up, each floret forming a small arrow which gets entangled in the hair, chiefly on the feet, with the base pointing towards the flesh. The seeds are so shaped that with the dog's movement they get drawn tighter to the skin, eventually causing a small hole to be rubbed between the toes or pads. The seeds should be removed as soon as they are discovered, and if a wound has already been started this should be treated with an antiseptic lotion. If the seed is left in, it is surprising how quickly it will disappear into the foot and seriously lame your dog. I have known a grass seed to penetrate the foot between the toes, and was not possible to extract it until it had reached the elbow. If you have the misfortune to get a seed really buried in your dog's foot it is advisable to get your veterinary surgeon to deal with it at once. Always remember that you must withdraw the seed from the front of the wound and not from the back; if drawn from the back you are liable to leave small particles behind, which will soon cause a festering sore. During the summer months it is always wise to brush and comb your dog after a country walk; by doing so you may save your dog much pain and yourself much worry.

Should the dog become badly infested with fleas or lice powder him thoroughly with insect powder. There are many dependable kinds to be had, but be careful of the eyes as certain preparations can be very harmful if they accidentally get into them. A wise plan is to fill the eye with a liberal supply of golden eye ointment before commencing the powdering. As soon as the dog has shaken himself this can be removed. As previously mentioned, no regularly groomed, well-kept dog should harbour livestock in his coat, so whatever else happens see to it that he is well-groomed and thoroughly looked over daily; the little time thus spent will well repay you. Dogs usually change their coats twice a year, in spring and autumn, but should they be in a run-down condition, or if bitches have been nursing puppies, they will lose their coats again. Feed on good raw beef, give plenty of exercise and again make sure your dog is regularly groomed. The accumulation of dirt and dust, as well as dandruff thrown off by the skin, is contrary to the maintenance of good health. Dogs are liable to pick up all sorts of germs and parasites on their coats, especially on the feet and lower part of the body. Therefore a dog's toilet should be as regular and equally as important as that of his master. I have so often heard owners say, "Go outside, you smelly dog," whereas if the poor little animal had been well cared for there would have been no need for such a remark. I am sorry to say that many people who own pets are under the impression that they require no attention to their personal cleanliness. Needless to say, this is a wrong idea; most dogs appreciate a daily brush and are so much better for it. Resentment is often due to the fact that the coat has been allowed to become matted, and a lot of rough handling and tugging is needed to get it in order again.

ELIZABETHAN COLLAR

An Elizabethan collar is a most useful asset to any Kennel. If you wish to prevent a dog from rubbing his eyes with his paws or, in the case of skin disease or any injured part, to stop him from licking or biting himself, I have found indispensable the collar I will describe. It is very simple to make. You will need some stiff cardboard or linoleum. Cut from this a circular piece about eighteen inches in diameter. Having done this, cut a hole in the centre big enough to fit comfortably round the dog's neck. Then remove a V-shaped piece, the top of the V being on the outer circumference. Fit it round the dog's neck and lace the two ends together with tape or string; for this purpose holes should be punched along the edges. The wide end of the collar should be well free from the side of the face. When it is being worn it should be the shape of a saucer.

EXERCISE

To keep a dog in really good health and hard condition it is essential he should be regularly exercised. Besides keeping the muscles of the body in tone exercise acts as a stimulant and tonic to the circulation and internal organs. In my opinion exercise is almost as important as good food, and should you intend to show your dog condition is one of the most important things in the show ring. Getting your dog into physical condition is something that cannot be done overnight; he will need weeks of hard, regular exercise, plus good food.

The fit dog has plenty of spirit, is keen and alert, full of the joy of living, and takes an interest in everything that is going on around him. The dog out of condition does not hold himself erect, he is listless, his coat is dull and lifeless, he is not interested in his surroundings, and in general he makes a very poor impression. He may have a large run or garden but that is not sufficient, and will not be the same as a scamper over the common, in the park or across country, with a thousand new smells. He is constantly sniffing adventure, laps at every stream and looks upon every

field as a new world to be explored—perhaps a few rabbits, a
woodcock, or a pheasant to put up. There is great value in the
mental change of all this delightful excitement. Dogs, like human
beings, need a change to keep fit. His mind needs feeding as well
as his body, and loneliness is irksome to him. To turn a dog into
the garden for an hour is useless; he will simply hang about the
gate waiting to be asked in, and if as fond of his food as most
cockers will be worried in case he is losing some tasty morsel in
the kitchen. Such strenuous exercise as following behind a horse
or a bicycle should not be allowed; it can be very injurious,
particularly if a dog is not in hard condition. During very hot
weather it is preferable, if possible, to give exercise in the early
morning or in the cool of the evening. Dogs should not be deprived
of their exercise because of inclement weather. Taking a dog out
in the rain will do no harm providing he is fit and is well rubbed
down on his return home. Be sure his coat is dry down to the skin—
the dog may be dry outwardly but probably near the skin the
hair is still damp. This is the thing that will bring on chills quicker
than anything, particularly if he is not used to getting wet. I find a
very useful thing for wet days is to keep a bath filled with sawdust.
Immediately you return from your walk the dog should be put
into this bath and thoroughly rubbed all over. The sawdust will
quickly absorb the damp and at the same time will remove the
mud. Take care that the dust does not get into the dog's eyes.
After you have rubbed him down turn him into a kennel filled
with straw, and it will be a joy to see how fresh and clean he will
be when you let him out later on. Should you live near the sea, a
daily swim will do no harm in warm weather, and most dogs
really enjoy one, but do not allow it if you have a show in view as
the salt water will remove all the show bloom you have put on.
An ordinary healthy dog can do with as much exercise as you can
give him within reason. If you are too busy to go for your usual
walk the dog will get a good deal of exercise in a short time if a
ball is thrown for him to retrieve.

TRIMMING

When you decide to show your dog you will need to start
getting the coat in order some weeks before the show. Begin by
giving a bath in a good shampoo. The next thing is to remove all

the dead coat; this should be done with finger and thumb, pullin
in the direction of the lay of the coat. Your task will be mad
easier when trimming if you rub your fingers with powdere
resin, or if you wear a thin rubber glove during the operatio
This will enable you to get a grip on the unwanted hair. On n
account resort to cutting; this would completely ruin the appea
ance of your dog. The scissored or knifed coat may look passabl
for the first week or so after it has been done but as soon as
starts to grow it will look a sorry sight. Also, it is against Kenne
Club rules and it is the duty of a judge to penalize such trimming
The only places on the dog where cutting is permissible are th
feet; there it will be necessary to cut out any dead hair, and t
trim the feet round.

When you remove the old coat, start at the head and remov
all the unwanted hair evenly—do not pluck out bits here an
there and make him look moth-eaten. Take out all the long hai
from behind the ears, proceed to do the neck and shoulders in th
same way and the surplus body coat; also well trim under th
tail. A lot of groundwork can be done with a No. 6 steel comb; con
stant combing and removal of dead hair will be a big help to
wards keeping a dog in show trim.

There is quite an art in preparing a cocker for the show rin
if you mean to exhibit him really well, and it will need years o
practice. I advise any novice who means to take up showin
seriously to gain experience from an expert; so much depends o
the trimming. A well-turned-out dog will look the part. You mus
not only know the way to trim; you must also know just where t
take it off. You should accentuate best points and try to minimiz
bad ones. When the trimming has been completed, regula
grooming will be necessary if you wish to maintain the smar
appearance needed for a show dog.

BATHING AND SHAMPOOING YOUR DOG

Although it is not wise to be unendingly bathing your dog, a
I have said in a previous Chapter, because too much bathing wil
remove the natural oil from the skin; on the other hand, it i
reasonable to assume that the house-dog will need to be washe
periodically for his own sake and that of everyone else concerned
A dog emanates body odours, particularly as it gets older, an

unless kept clean can be most unpleasant. I find an easy way of bathing a dog is to stand it on the draining-board next to the kitchen sink, which you fill with water. You can then pour the water over the dog until he is thoroughly wet; the soap is then applied and rubbed into a good lather. It is more simple to wash the leg featherings and feet in this way. Care should be taken to avoid soap getting into the eyes. When the dog has been well rubbed all over immerse him in the sink and rinse thoroughly. On being removed allow him to shake himself to get rid of the greater part of the water on his coat. For drying I find a chamois leather invaluable. Wring the leather out in warm water and rub thoroughly with it. By this method one can get the dog practically dry, ready to finish off with a hot towel. Getting the coat back into place can be simplified by combing the dog in front of a fire, while he is still damp. During the very cold weather a spirituous dry shampoo may be used; most dog shops can supply a shampoo of this sort. Also, there are many forms of cleaning blocks to be had. A somewhat more pleasant cleaning preparation is ordinary talcum powder; rub well in, then thoroughly brush out and finish off with a dry, soft, clean chamois leather. Your dog will be fresh and sweet after this.

Should your dog be scratching himself, and you are sure the cause is not "livestock", a valuable remedy can be made up by dissolving one ounce of sulphurated potash to a pail of tepid water, in which solution the dog may be immersed for about ten to fifteen minutes.

Do not let a dog go out and lie about on a cold day just after a bath. When he is thoroughly dry he should be encouraged to lie in his box or basket, which should be in a place selected because of freedom from draughts. It is not wise to bath an old or delicate dog during cold weather. Just as human beings, some are tough and can stand almost anything, whereas others are very susceptible to chills. A bitch in season should definitely not be bathed and you should make certain she is quite normal before attempting to do so.

HOUSING

There are many types of kennels in use; pattern is a matter of choice, but the health of the inmates depends considerably on the building in which they are housed. Stables and loosoxes make be ideal kennels if each dog is given a warm sleeping box raised on short legs, or a bench, as stable flooring is mostly stone or concrete and very cold. Dogs, like human beings, need a comfortable bed. I have heard many breeders say that dogs should not be molly-coddled. I am all for making my dogs comfortable and you will find, if given a fresh straw bed, dogs will be contented. The straw should be renewed at least once a week. Old carpets and sacks, which harbour insects, dust and damp, are very objectionable. Hay is also poor bedding as it becomes foul and sodden. No artificial heat is necessary for strong, healthy dogs. Any cocker can live in comfort in an outside kennel of the right type; it is the fireside dog that is more liable to catch cold. Timber kennels are very successful, being comparatively cheap to build, but these should be lined with boarding or asbestos sheeting. It is a good idea also to line the doors with sheet tin or zinc, as dogs like to bite out if they can and will very quickly ruin a kennel door, and the splinters of wood which they may swallow can be very harmful. Kennels should be light and free from draughts. Plenty of fresh air is necessary to keep dogs fit. Windows should be made to open, but they must be placed as high as possible, so that there is no likelihood of the dogs jumping out. If there are at least two windows, one at each end of the kennel, they can be opened together, which will allow a current of air to pass through and take away any doggy smells.

One of the most popular types of kennels is a range where several dogs can be kept under one roof, with a passage-way under cover where one can move about in wet weather. Size depends on the number of dogs kept. Such a kennel will need an open-air run as large as space will permit. It is wise to place a bench or two in the run where dogs can lie out of the damp if they are inclined to sleep. If it is possible to construct your run so that it encloses a tree the dogs will appreciate this in the hot, glaring sun of summer. I have a weeping willow in my run, which I purposely had planted for the dogs, and they just love it on very hot days, when they can relax in the cool. These trees are very quick growing, and if you are just beginning to construct your kennels it is really worth while planting one; apart from being decorative, the dogs will thank you for it in summer days.

A constant supply of pure, fresh drinking water is a recognized necessity for the healthy dog. It must never be neglected. It is wise to change this two or three times a day during hot weather.

The drinking vessels, as also the feeding dishes, should be kept scrupulously clean.

I strongly advise that the kennel kitchen is situated away from the other buildings, to save all risk of fire. It should be erected well away from any hen runs—the scattered food will attract rats. The kitchen can be a small building of corrugated iron sheets, with a boiler and a table for cutting up the meat. I find a good farm boiler or sawyer stove very useful, although some people prefer a pressure cooker. The floor should be of concrete, in order that it can be easily washed down. Kennels should always be kept spotless; no dust, dirt or rejected food should be allowed to remain.

When the dogs are let out for their early morning run all soiled bedding and sawdust should be removed and replaced with fresh; sawdust is wholesome and best for all kennel floors. This can be obtained from any saw-mills, but be sure it is fine and not filled with splinters. A thick layer should be spread over the floor of all kennels, particularly if they are concrete floors, as it is warm and absorbent. It is useful to have a small incinerator tucked away in some corner, where droppings, old bedding and sawdust can be burnt. Once every week the kennels should be thoroughly turned out and scrubbed through with a good disinfectant. It is advisable to do this in the morning, so that the kennels have time to dry thoroughly before the dogs are put into them at night. Runs also need regularly cleaning and any droppings should be picked up. Should you have a kennel where there has been any infectious disease it must be thoroughly scrubbed with a strong disinfectant, not forgetting the walls and ceilings. When thoroughly dry, seal every crack and crevice to make it airtight, then place in an old tin or bucket two pounds of powdered sulphur—this should be sufficient for a kennel about twenty feet square; proportionate quantities for larger or smaller kennels —pour a couple of tablespoonfuls of methylated spirits over the sulphur and ignite it. Close the door quickly, seal any cracks at the edges, then leave for at least twenty-four hours. Another good way of eradicating germs is to run a blow-lamp over the woodwork; this method will dispose of all forms of infection. When the kennels are thoroughly disinfected or fumigated it is wise to open door and windows and leave to the weather for two or three months before introducing another dog.

Do not forget to disinfect your brushes, combs, collars, leads

F

and everything connected with the dogs and kennel. They are all germ traps.

PURCHASING A PUPPY

There is a marked increase in the desire to own a cocker spaniel as a pet. As you go through the suburban districts of London almost every second dog you see is a cocker. This goes to show their popularity and adaptability. They are equally happy in town or country, if given their daily walk. In every town there are parks or commons where dogs can be exercised and have a good scamper off the lead. When you decide to buy your puppy too much importance cannot be attached to selecting a healthy specimen. Make sure of getting one that will bring no regrets; you are buying a pet and you want to enjoy it, so do not attempt to buy a weed because it is half the price of the others. You will be taking on trouble and in the end it will cost you more in vet's bills than you paid for it. A healthy puppy will repay you time and time again. If it is to become only a companion a typical specimen is all that is necessary, but even so it is wise to choose one from a really good strain, as everyone likes to feel the dog he cherishes is a good-looking one and a badly bred puppy so often grows into an ugly duckling. This is such a disappointment to his owner, as even if it is not intended for show he likes it to look attractive and to feel proud of it when they go walking together. The safest person from whom to buy a puppy is the breeder. In my opinion a bitch will make the best companion. She will need a little extra care, about twice a year for three weeks when she is in season, but she will be no trouble providing you do not keep a dog. I should not advise a bitch if you already have a dog; this would be asking for trouble.

If you are interested in showing and feel you would like to try your luck in the show ring I would advise you to put yourself in the hands of a reliable breeder and buy the best you can afford, but faultless puppies are very difficult to come by and usually a breeder will want to keep his very best puppies to show himself. Before getting your puppy, if you have had no experience of this kind of thing and are at a loss to know how to make a start, there are many open and championship shows during the year which one can attend to gain knowledge, and there you can decide on the colour and type you prefer. Exhibitors are usually very helpful to newcomers, so get to know a breeder who will, I am sure, be only too glad to help you and will no doubt make arrangements for you to visit his Kennels with a view to selecting a suitable puppy. It would probably be possible for you to see the parents and grandparents whilst you are there; this would give you an idea as to how your puppy is likely to appear when fully grown. If you are unable to get to any shows, you will probably be able to find what you are looking for advertised in the dog papers. Genuine breeders are always delighted to welcome visitors at their Kennels, providing an appointment is made. Dealing by letter is not always satisfactory unless you actually know the people you are doing business with. Some advertisers will describe very mediocre specimens as certain champions; no one is going to sell a dog which looks like being a champion unless he gets a fabulous price for it, so do not attach any importance to these glowing advertisements. Also, before making your final decision to purchase have a copy of the pedigree sent to you, and if you are in doubt as to whether it is correct the Kennel Club will verify it for you. When the puppy arrives, if you are not too happy about its health have it examined by your veterinary surgeon. This can be done for quite a reasonable fee. If, after examination, you find it is not in good health communicate immediately with the sender and arrange to return it to him. It seems hard luck for the poor little puppy but it is the only thing to do.

If the puppy comes up to expectations and you keep it, the next thing to do is to register it at the Kennel Club. This, of course, is not essential, but if you intend to use it for breeding or showing at any time it will need to be registered. If the puppy has already been registered the new owner must get it transferred into his or her name. Transfers must also be registered at the Kennel Club.

For the first couple of days after arrival the puppy will possibly feel very strange and he will be a bit suspicious and unresponsive. If he has come from a Kennel he will miss his companions and will be very homesick and may cry a lot at night, but if he is given a good meal, treated kindly and made comfortable, he will soon settle down, particularly if he knows friends are not far away.

SELLING A PUPPY

When you have puppies for sale decide as early as possible which you intend to run on for show or breeding and let the remainder go as soon as practicable. The longer you keep them, the more they will cost you; therefore it will pay you to let the surplus go for what you can get, within reason, thus avoiding profit being eaten up. Never sell a dog showing any signs of illness or skin trouble. Should you do so it will cause you more worry than the worth of the puppy and in the end it will no doubt be returned to you. Also, it is so unkind to send a poor little animal away to a strange home unless it is a hundred per cent fit. On no account let your puppies go on approval. Once out of your hands you never know what infection they might pick up, and should a puppy be returned you may lose half your Kennel in consequence; puppies quickly take any disease that is going about. Invite your client to your Kennel; it is much more satisfactory to you both, and puppies are always at their best in their own surroundings.

Issue a diet sheet with every puppy you sell and hand it over with the pedigree. So many puppies go wrong immediately they have left the care of the breeder, owing to wrong feeding or, more often than not, being overfed. A healthy puppy is naturally greedy and will always be asking for more. If he is given as much as he asks for he will become upset inside and the buyer will at once think he has been sold an ill puppy, when actually it is nothing more than the outcome of an unsuitable diet—and too much of it.

Unless you are known in the dog world and have a ready sale for all your stock an advertisement in the general press or your local paper is the best way to dispose of your puppies. Do not misrepresent them, avoid over-statement, and always remember that the thing to aim at is a reputation for reliable dealing. Satisfied purchasers tell others. And it is the best form of advertisement; as time goes on you will become successful in your dog business and quickly dispose of your stock. You will make many friends, too, and how proud you will feel when your puppies are brought back to see you and their owners say, "I wouldn't sell him back to you for double the money." I always get great joy out of such a remark. Although it is the right thing to give everyone value for his money, I am equally against giving puppies away. How often I have heard said, "I am only mating my bitch as my vet says it will be good for her to have a litter, but I shall not sell the puppies—I would rather give them away to good homes." I always think this rather a stupid remark, as in my opinion this is when they are likely to find bad homes. If people are real dog lovers they will already have a dog, and if they cannot afford a pure bred one they will be happy with a mongrel. So often the dogless person will accept a puppy because it is offered for nothing. They just love it as a baby; it will be so cute and amusing, it will probably have lovely long ears and such a doleful expression and everyone in the family will give it endless attention. But as it grows older and loses its attractiveness it will possibly become a poor, neglected, unwanted dog. I have seen this happen so many times. Eventually it may be given away to anyone who cares to have it, or even turned out into the street to fend for itself. Another thing I have come up against: all is well until the poor unfortunate puppy is ill; the owner at once finds it is quite impossible to keep it and it is brought back to you with endless apologies and excuses. So my advice is: never give a puppy away unless you know the people well and they have already had a dog.

Training the House Pet

Dogs, like human beings, have different temperaments, each individual having a distinct personality. Some are instinctively more responsive than others. No two dogs are alike in looks or character. Some are more quickly trained than others. The trainer will need to be patient and understanding; he will also need to be kind but at the same time firm. Should a dog be needed either as a house pet or as a show dog training should commence at an early age. A well-trained dog is a pleasure, an unruly one a nuisance.

Presuming your puppy is to be a pet in the house, his first lesson will be cleanliness. Make him understand that he must not misbehave himself; his favourite place will be your carpets. If he is allowed the run of the house, keep him away from your best rooms until he has learnt what is expected of him. Put him outside at the slightest hint that he is about to misbehave himself, also immediately after meals and first thing in the morning and last thing at night. A dog's memory is wonderfully retentive, and when he has thoroughly learnt a lesson he will not easily forget it. Cleanliness in flats is a difficult situation because it is not possible to turn your pet into a garden. I have often heard of puppies being successfully trained on a galvanized tray. The tray should be filled with sawdust and the puppy put on it several times a day, particularly after meals. He will quickly learn what is needed of him. When he becomes old enough to be taken for walks the tray can be done away with.

There are other house manners to be learnt. If you allow your dog to be present at meals, do not give him tit-bits. If you once start he will give you no peace until he has eaten almost every-thing on the table. I have yet to meet a cocker who is not always hungry; even if they have just eaten a big meal they will still tell you they are starving, so if yours persists in worrying for food shut him out of the room. Being a sensible dog he will soon get to know why he has been turned out. Another bad habit, if he is not checked, will be to jump on chairs and scratch up cushions, and perhaps shower the place with feathers. Then he will come to the door to meet you, looking very innocent, with eathers stuck all over his nose. I have had this happen on more than one occasion. Another important thing is not to allow your dog to jump up; there is nothing more annoying than to be jumped at and pawed over each time you enter the house. He may seriously damage your best suit, or ruin your silk stockings. To come home and meet your dog should be a pleasurable experience, not one necessitating changing into old clothes before you dare make an appearance. Good manners in the road should also be taught; do not allow him to foul the pavements—you can always guide him into the gutter. Teach your puppy to walk quietly on the lead; he will probably want to run ahead and pull at the lead. Correct this at once. Nothing looks worse than to see the dog taking you for a walk instead of you taking him. Try to get him to walk just behind to your left; your task will be more simple if you carry some tasty tit-bit in your left hand and reward him occasionally. If your puppy sits down and refuses to walk at all do not pull him. Just get behind him and give him a pat; he will soon start off again. You can also train him to follow off the lead when required, but even the best-behaved dogs are safer attached to a lead when in a busy thoroughfare. Inevitably one day he will see a dog on the other side of the road, or more likely a cat, and will probably forget his training in his excitement and dart into the road and under a car or bus. I have seen it happen many times. Dogs are so often blamed for bad behaviour when it is usually the fault of the owner; if a dog is not well trained he will always be a nuisance. A cocker is a very faithful animal and is always anxious to please; therefore the greatest kindness his owner can do is to spend a little time in training him. He will be well rewarded; his friendship and devout affection are well worth cultivating.

If you consider him and treat him with the kindness he deserves you can have no better companion; he will almost know your thoughts, he will always be the same faithful little friend, whatever sort of mood you may be in, and will unfailingly greet you with a wag of the tail.

I have often been asked, "Is it fair to make a pet of a cocker, as he is a sporting dog?" My answer is, "Yes." Most breeds originate from sporting stock, and if a cocker is given plenty of exercise and companionship he will be happy. On the other hand, there is commonsense in all things; for instance, it would be unfair to take a working cocker who had been regularly shot over and expect him to be happy in a London flat.

If you keep poultry you should let your puppy know from an early age they are not to be molested. They are a great temptation to a young cocker; he will probably start by chasing them and pulling their tail feathers out, which will be great fun, but if this is not checked in the beginning you will probably go out one day and find all your hens killed. The same principles apply to chasing deer or sheep. If treated with a very firm hand at the start he will probably make a peace pact with all these and grow up to respect them. You will then be able to meet them with a free mind when out for your walk together. To my way of thinking there is no greater embarrassment than for an owner to take his dog where there are deer or sheep and suddenly find him giving chase with a herd or a flock ahead of him. Apart from the embarrassment, it is a serious offence. A real dog lover will find training less difficult. Dogs are gifted with a wonderful instinct which enables them to know their friends. This explains why people who are genuine dog lovers have more success in training and showing. Dogs put their trust in them and try to do everything they can to please. I feel one can often judge people's characters by their attitude towards animals, and those timid individuals who dislike and are afraid of dogs must not be surprised if they get bitten; dogs can quickly recognize enemies and are not above giving them a quiet nip. Dog-loving people who have an intimate knowledge of canine character seldom get bitten; they are usually given a welcome.

Dogs kept chained up often become very ferocious. You cannot blame them. If I were a dog kept on a chain I should bite everything on sight! Just think of it: every day on the end of a chain, day in and day out. I am sorry to say one will often see this in the country, the poor dog frequently without water, a dirty little crust thrown down for a meal, no one to say a friendly word, and kept for the sole purpose of giving warning of an approaching stranger. In time the system becomes weakened and the mind becomes numb, the outcome of an existence of lasting solitude. Nothing could be more cruel and any dog lover should fight against this cruelty by reporting such cases to the R.S.P.C.A.

Some people go to the other extreme and allow their dog to curl up and sleep on their bed. I think this is wrong. It is unhygienic and should the owner become ill the dog must find another sleeping place. He will be utterly miserable and unsettled; a cocker is a great one for routine where his bit of comfort is concerned. If you must have him in your room at night let him have his own basket, which will be much better for both owner and dog.

The Novice Exhibitor

When you begin dog showing go about your business very quietly, taking every opportunity of learning all you can by watching the successful exhibitor. Should you get to the show early, do not stand at the bench of a well known exhibitor waiting for him to arrive and as soon as you set eyes on him ask a thousand questions—a typical one is: "Which one is this?" and "Will you tell me what you think of my dog?" before the exhibitor has had time to get his dogs on the bench or shake himself out. He will probably have had a long journey and will be a bit on edge, so wait until he has got his dogs settled and then he will no doubt be only too pleased to tell you all you want to know. When it is nearing your time to enter the show ring, take your dog off his bench and give him the last-minute brush and comb. Keep your mind on your job, first, last, and always. Memorize the number of your first class; be ready to walk into the ring as soon as your class comes along; do not remain talking to everyone and over-look your class. Above all, do not have to be sent for; it is very annoying to the stewards to have to go searching round the benches and calling out your number, and also to your fellow exhibitors as it will hold everyone up, which, apart from everything else, is not etiquette as there are such things as ring manners. When you eventually get into the ring do not gaze absentmindedly about you; keep your thoughts on your dog the whole time until the cards are given out. See that he is standing in his most attractive position: the judge might give him a side glance and catch him at an awkward angle, which might lose you the card he had in mind for you. Also, do not call the judge's notice to a fault by trying to conceal or minimize it. Should you not win anything do not go to the judge and tell him what you won at another show; perhaps the competition was not so keen on the day you won, and this judge might l ke a different type. It is a poor sort of judge who has no mind of his own and has to follow the placings of others or assess a dog on past performances. Should the appointed judge happen to be a friend of yours do not pretend, when you get to the show, never to have seen him before—he will think more of you if you just pass the time of day—and do not expect to receive awards with inferior specimens because you are a friend. Re-member there are many judges sitting at the ring-side, and a judge can quickly lose his reputation by "putting up" poor specimens because they belong to friends. Never be disheartened if you do not win; study the winners closely and find out what is wrong with your dog. Maybe you have not trimmed him correctly, or perhaps he has not been taught what is needed of him in the show ring.

A beginner would be wise to avoid big shows until experience has been gained. At the smaller local shows competition is not so keen; confidence can be gained and a lot learnt in the way of handling. I have often heard a novice say that he showed his dog but could not win a thing with him. Such people make up their minds that it is useless going on, so decide to sell. A dog is sold to a famous Kennel and immediately he is shown he goes to the top, but it never occurs to the original owner that the ex-perienced breeder has made a close study of training, handling and trimming. The dog with his new owner is trained to go into the ring with a gay appearance, is taught to stand and show off his best points, and is trimmed to perfection. A well-turned-out dog is able to cover many shortcomings in other points, for there is yet to be bred the cocker every judge will acclaim as perfect. If you have a good dog and he is put into the ring as he should be, his day will come, whoever the owner may be.

A novice need not feel he is a nobody in the show ring; he is the backbone of the dog world; without him shows would not go on. All exhibitors are only too pleased to welcome recruits if they have the love of their breed at heart. Needless to say, most breeders have.

Dog shows are of four different types: Championship, Open, Limited, and Sanction shows. A show of Championship status is the most important of all and is authorized by the Kennel Club to award Challenge Certificates. With most breeds, when a dog has won three certificates under three different judges such a winner is classed as a champion, but it is not so with gundogs—they must pass a field test before being allowed to use the title. The cocker spaniel is one of the gundog group. Therefore it is necessary to obtain a qualifying certificate at a recognized Field Trial in accordance with Kennel Club rules before one can obtain the title of Champion.[1] Open and Limited Shows are held under licence of the Kennel Club. At an Open Show anyone can compete, but when Limited it is confined to Clubs or Societies within specified areas. A Sanction Show is restricted to twenty-five classes, and is ideal for the novice to make a start, as at a show of this type the tension is not so great and much knowledge can be gained. It is also a useful show for the less ambitious exhibitor.

Bear in mind that dog showing is a form of competitive sport and should be taken as such. Do not listen to all the bits of tittle-tattle you will be certain to hear. When I was quite a novice there came to my hearing an unkind remark someone had made about my dog. I was greatly hurt and spoke to our greatest cocker authority about it. His answer was: "Don't worry. You can take it as the greatest compliment; if your dog was a bad one they wouldn't bother to talk about him." I have always remembered this and it has helped me many times; so now when I hear that one of my dogs is being talked about unkindly I feel considerable satisfaction and know the dog has "caught on". Fortunately for most of us, all these little bits of scandal when investigated boil down to nothing; they usually come from a disgruntled exhibitor who has had a bad day, or from a newcomer to the breed who repeats hearsay he has accepted as fact.

[1] *See* Addendum, page 141.

Another thing you often hear is that the poor unfortunate novice will never stand a chance of winning, however good his dog may be. This of course is nonsense; if his dog is good enough he will certainly win. At the time of writing two comparatively novice exhibitors have had most sensational wins—both have won Challenge Certificates. So do not get disheartened if you have a good dog. Keep showing him, remembering all the well-known exhibitors of today were once beginners, and sure enough your day will come. When you have been fortunate enough to breed a dog worthy of winning a Challenge Certificate, and one that is sought after for stud, you have achieved something which all breeders are aiming at. It has probably been the outcome of many years' hard work and concentration, but you have reached your goal and it has been well worth all the heartbreaks and setbacks you no doubt endured.

TRAINING FOR THE SHOW RING

You can commence training your puppy for the show ring very early in his life; even at the tender age of eight or ten weeks you can train him to stand—mastering this is a good start and should make the more serious training less difficult. Between the age of five or six months is quite soon enough to introduce him to the lead. Should he not take kindly to it, no attempt should be made to pull him. The lead should be kept fairly loose at first, or attach it to his collar and let him drag it about where he pleases. Finally, retain the lead in your hand and allow him to move at his own will—he will soon become accustomed to it. I have found that another successful way of training a puppy is to take him out with the adult dogs. He will be so intent on following them that he will completely forget he is being led.

Assuming your puppy is trained to the lead, now is the time to begin lessons for the show ring. Make sure you have your dog's attention, and reward good behaviour with a tit-bit. Simulate or reproduce in your own run, or in any surroundings to which the dog is accustomed, as near as possible the actual show ring, even to the extent of having a stranger to handle him, which can often be arranged when a friend calls. When you have everything in order, attach him to a slip lead and put him through his paces, walk him round the home-made ring, pose and re-pose him, run him up and down the centre of the ring, and set him up again;

and then get your friend, who is a stranger to the dog, to handle him as though he or she were the judge. If your puppy is sensible and free from nerves lessons of this sort every day for a week should be sufficient for him to know what is wanted. Firm nerves and self-possession are essential qualities in the show ring for both exhibit and exhibitor. Many good dogs leave the ring cardless owing to bad showing, due to nervousness. Should the handler be nervous in the ring, I am confident the nervousness can be transmitted through the lead to the dog, so you cannot expect your dog to be a fearless shower if you are all het up with nerves. After all, there is nothing to be nervous about—the onlookers are looking at your dog, not at you. I have met many novice exhibitors who become self-conscious immediately they enter the ring and this at once reflects on a dog.

The dog in training should be taken into crowds, particularly if owners live in quiet country districts, where their dogs are not used to meeting a lot of people. Your pupil should be taken through traffic and in the midst of noise; also, take him into any of the big stores. The trainer must have great patience and, above all, persistent kindness. He should use a quiet voice; dogs dislike being shouted at. Some dogs seem to be born with a natural aptitude for showing, others learn only by experience or have to be taught. Do not imagine that a perfectly trained dog will remain so if badly handled.

Having got your dog trained as you want him, you may enter him at a show. He will need to be in good condition; he must be firm with plenty of muscle but not fat; lean meat and plenty of exercise are in my opinion the best things for getting a dog into condition. When you have decided on your show send a postcard to the secretary asking for a schedule, if you have not already received one. He will be only too pleased to send you one by return. All shows are advertised in the dog papers for some time before the entries close. When the schedule arrives the next thing is to enter your dog to the best advantage. The definition of the different classes will be seen at the beginning of the schedule. These classes are so arranged that dogs which have done a certain amount of winning cannot enter in the lower classes, therefore your puppy will not have to compete with the well-known winners unless you unwisely enter him in the higher classes, which would be a great mistake on your first attempt. Also, a puppy has very little chance of winning when he is competing against mature dogs. Your policy should be to enter him in classes where you think he may stand a chance of being in the first three; perhaps you could get advice from a regular exhibitor with your first entry.

When the show day arrives make a point of reaching there quite half an hour before the scheduled time for judging. The next thing is to find your bench, which will be numbered. When you have settled your dog in, discover the location of the cocker ring; this will avoid searching at the last minute, which might mean missing your class. Then a good grooming can be done, so that the dog will be ready when your class comes along. When you are at long last in the ring you will have been given a ring number, which you attach to yourself where it can be easily seen. Exhibitors will then be asked to move their dogs round the ring. Always keep the dog on your left side, that is, in full view of the judge, taking care not to tread on the heels of the person or the dog in front of you. The judge and the ring stewards must be obeyed; if you are asked to stand in a certain position or order, stay there until you are wanted again. When you are asked to move your dog, take him up and back briskly, in the direction in which the judge wants it moved. It will be chiefly the dog's action he will be looking at. Sound movement will play a big part in the placing of your dog in the prize list; so many are good standing and will look the winner, but when they are asked to move—oh, dear, what a disappointment! If the movement is bad it will stop the dog, however good in other points, getting very high in the awards, particularly if competition is keen. The standard of the cocker is so high today that a bad mover will not be tolerated. Therefore too much attention cannot be paid to the movement of your prospective prize winner. Movement should give a clue to the general make and shape; there should be perfect freedom at shoulder, elbow, stifle and hock. The gait should be easy and straightforward, each leg swinging forth and back the same distance forwards as it does backwards. Turned-in toes (known as pintoes), any side swing of either leg or foot, are to be deplored, as is also any upward swing of the forefeet or any action similar to that of a hackney pony. Style is inborn and cannot be taught, but every dog can be trained to show the best style of which he is capable.

When the awards are given out, accept whatever they may be with a good heart; if your dog is not placed do not be disappointed. Dog showing will lose all its joy if you allow a bad day to worry you. After all, there will be another day and another judge who will perhaps like your dog better, as some judges like an entirely different type.

The decision of the judge is absolutely final. It is useless to make a fuss; this only makes you look unsporting, so however disappointed you may feel it is better to say nothing, as complaining will not help matters. You have taken your dog to the show of your own free will, for the judge's criticism, so you must accept it. If you do not agree with the placings, or if you are anxious to know why your dog was turned down, go up to the judge quietly after he has finished his judging and ask the reason. A judge will be only too pleased to tell you, providing you approach him in the right way; he will no doubt comment on the qualities and failings of your dog. Remember his criticism; it will greatly help you in the future.

Another very important thing to remember is the handling of your exhibit in the show ring. So much depends on this; a good handler can show off his dog to the best advantage and bring out his good points, whilst a bad handler can manage to disguise the good points of the very same dog. Other things being equal, the dog shown by an experienced handler will often beat the one in the hands of the inexperienced one, simply because the novice has not learnt the art of handling, and his dog has not been seen to the best advantage. I have sometimes judged at country shows, where you meet a lot of novice exhibitors, and have discovered that when you try to handle some dogs they flatly refuse to be handled. Often they will not even stand on their four legs, and when asked to move they simply rush across the ring with their tails tucked beneath them, and their ears on top of their heads, looking in all directions. It is quite impossible to sum up a dog of this sort, and a judge is not to blame if an otherwise good specimen fails to get placed. So if you intend to take up showing make a point of knowing what is expected of your dog in the ring; it is of the greatest importance to accustom him to show himself off and to be at his natural best in the show ring.

AFTER THE SHOW

For several days after bringing a young dog back from a show he should be carefully watched, and should he appear languid, with an indifferent appetite, or the development of a temperature, professional advice should be sought. It is in fact a wise precaution to isolate after a show for at least a week, particularly when you have young dogs in your kennel. This will often save the introduction of infection amongst your other stock. On the other hand, the exhibitor would do well to have his dogs immunized against distemper before attending a show, as this disease is the major risk involved. It must be admitted dog shows have their drawbacks, but the dog would never have reached its present high standard without them. The show is the only way the breeder has of showing off his stock, and without the endorsement of our judges the British Cocker would never have gained a world-wide reputation and attained its present popularity.

NERVOUSNESS IN SHOW DOGS

Many dogs suffer with nerves, and a veterinary surgeon cannot do much to help in such cases as medicinal treatment does little good. I have heard it said many times that highly bred show dogs are so often nervous, but I wonder if this is due to dogs not having being taken out until they became adults. Owners of valuable show dogs are so afraid of taking them out and picking up some infection. As a consequence, during puppyhood they see only little of the outside world, whereas an ordinary puppy purchased as a pet is immediately familiarized with strange sights and noises, taken amongst traffic, meeting different people and all sorts of dogs; therefore they seldom suffer with nerves. If you wish to conquer nerves you should take it in hand during puppyhood. One is sorry to see so many nervous dogs at the shows nowadays, and I do regret to say it is becoming more prevalent: tails tucked beneath them, for example, and no sign of the merry cocker wriggle which has always been so characteristic of the breed.

I think judges should penalize this very severely as, if it is allowed to go on, our little cocker will lose all its charm. Tail wagging is a particular fetish of mine; I regard it as a most valuable asset to a show cocker. I am almost certain this tucked-in tail is the result of puppies having being kept in safe seclusion for too long. Let your puppies meet people and take them into traffic at an early age, even if you carry them under your arms. Were such a policy general I am sure we should see fewer nervous dogs in the show ring. It is worth a little risk. If I have a couple of promising puppies which I intend to run on I often put them in the car when I go shopping. They usually dislike it at first but I find that after the first two or three times they really enjoy it, particularly if you give them some tasty morsel once or twice during the journey. If your puppy is eventually to become a show dog it is certainly worth the little extra time spent in such training. Nothing can be more distressing to an owner than to arrive at a dog show with his exhibit absolutely petrified with nerves. Both finish up by having a miserable day, and the owner feels that he never wants to see another dog show, having got nowhere in the award list. I have, fortunately, never owned a nervous dog, and I am quite sure this is only because I get mine out early in life. Dogs are often just what you make them. The cocker, like all dogs, is a highly sensitive animal and, as I have said before, like human beings each has an individual temperament. You cannot treat them all alike.

All dogs dislike being handled roughly and by so doing a good-tempered dog can be quickly turned into a bad-tempered, nervous one. If you treat your dog kindly he will have complete trust in you, and once you have gained his confidence you create a duty never to let him down. Cockers are wonderfully loyal and I am sorry to say often lavish their affections on unworthy masters. Owners should return their dogs' devotion and the faith and trust put in them. It is the duty of all breeders to see that the right kind of people acquire their dogs. The British are a dog-loving people, but even so we have too many dogs in the hands of the wrong kind of owners. The dog for many hundreds, perhaps thousands, of years has been in close association with mankind. The right kind of human companionship has become essential to his mental well-being and not even the company of his own kind can take its place. The more, therefore, one's cockers are about with one the better it is for them and the more intelligent they will become. When in Kennels they should have the companionship of other dogs and, if possible, an outside run where they can see everything that is going on. It is a great mistake to tuck show dogs away where they never see anyone yet expect them to go to a dog show, meeting hundreds of strange people, without a sign of a nerve. If you hope to exhibit a dog and do well with him it will pay you to take him out as much as you can amongst people.

The author with Sh. Ch. Sixshot Sugar Bird at the Manchester Championship Show 1952

The Sixshots

Bronze Turkey, Goldfinch, Black Grouse, Black Swan, and Brown Owl

Ch. Golden Rod of Ide

Ch. Lochranza Latch Key

Sh. Ch. Glendorgal Spritely Lad

The dog, being a highly sensitive animal with an acute instinct for self-protection, will often snap at strangers if he is nervous and highly strung and has not been in the habit of meeting many people. If he does this in the show ring, however good he may be the judge will not place him. A nervous dog will require careful treatment, and a great deal of time and patience is sometimes necessary to educate them to sense kindness.

An Intelligent Dog

I have so often heard people say, "Oh, give me a mongrel every time for intelligence and companionship." With this I cannot altogether agree. Although I do not wish to belittle the intelligence of the mongrel, nor have I any criticism to make regarding its devotion to its master, I have at different times owned some amazingly clever cocker spaniels. I once had a red cocker bitch named Plum, and she really was one of the most intelligent dogs I ever knew, for she used all her senses—in fact she was almost human. It was during a very hot summer's day, when the temperature was over 80 degrees, and she was nursing a litter of puppies. Each time I visited her I found the puppies soaking wet, which really puzzled me until I actually caught her in the act of dipping one into her water bowl. I was so amazed that I just stood and watched her whilst she returned the puppy to the nest and treated each of the others in the same manner, and finished by making herself as wet as possible. They did look an uncomfortable little lot by the time she had finished, but the procedure made me realize the common sense this little mother had got. She knew her puppies were too hot, so decided to make them cool. Needless to say, her water bowl was promptly removed.

Life, however, is the sum of things which one remembers, and when I look back and review the clever things this little cocker did I have little desire to argue whether she worked by instinct or reason.

All dogs like eggs, and eggs have a pleasant smell in their nostrils. More than this, they seem instinctively to know they are of a brittle nature and need handling carefully. Each time my little bitch heard the cackling of a hen she would rush to the henhouse and wait at the gate to be let in. When I opened the gate she would go forth, collect the egg and bring it out in a most care-

G

ful manner and lay it in my hand. She would then give one sharp little bark and go in and collect another, and so on until all the eggs in the nests had been brought to me. But alas! in the end she disgraced herself. It was not always convenient to be there to open the gate; the hens would cackle and she must get in at all costs so she commenced digging under the wire. Then we could not understand why there were no eggs. We knew the hens were in full lay; perhaps the rats were taking them. I went to investigate and found a sprinkling of egg shells in the hen-house, and then I noticed that Plum's ears were covered with yellow, which looked uncommonly like the yolk of an egg. This was indeed very suspicious. She knew she had done wrong and her brown eyes looked up with an appeal that no sentiment can exaggerate. I immediately forgave her, although I told her she would never in all her life be allowed to collect the eggs again.

Dogs certainly possess what we call a conscience—that is, they are well aware when they have done wrong, and everyone who has kept cockers will have little doubt about the profound depth of their affection. Plum's instinct would always tell her when I was nearing home, and she would be waiting to welcome me with the utmost importance, wearing a broad smile, twisting her lips and showing her teeth. This was another of her marked characteristics. To the rest of the world she was rather indifferent, though always perfectly courteous and polite to everybody. She had a striking personality; she used to sit up for everything she wanted, although she had never been taught to do so as I am not in favour of dogs doing tricks. When Plum was six years of age she left us. This was a very sad day and marred my pleasure for some time. We had accepted an invitation to dine with friends that night but asked to be excused owing to the death of a "dear little friend".

Essentials for the Novice to Remember

Fresh, clean water should always be available. On no account ever chain your cocker up; it is a cruel practice. One cannot imagine any dog-loving person doing such a thing, but I am sorry to say that, much to my horror, I once found a puppy I had sold being treated this way. I promptly bought the poor darling back and found him a home where he was appreciated. If it is not convenient to let him have his full liberty build a run of some kind for him.

Always keep your kennels and feeding bowls scrupulously clean. A dog will not be healthy in a dirty kennel.

Brush and comb your dog daily and see that he is free from livestock. Don't forget that dirt will encourage fleas and skin disease.

A large raw bone is good for dogs of all ages, but never give game, poultry, rabbit or chop bones as they are liable to splinter and cause serious internal trouble.

Too much sloppy food upsets a cocker's inside and deprives his digestive organs of their exercise. Never overfeed or underfeed your dog; two good meals a day at regular times are sufficient.

Should you own only one house pet and be unfortunate enough to lose it by distemper, do not buy another for several months unless it has already had this disease; the infection may remain in your house and be passed on to the new arrival. Distemper is very infectious and can be carried even on your clothing.

If you have several dogs do not show favouritism to one and neglect the others.

Never overcrowd; do not have more dogs than your Kennel and grounds will take comfortably.

Well ventilate your kennel; cockers need plenty of fresh air; as do human beings; germs thrive in bad ventilation.

See that your dog has daily exercise, which he will greatly look forward to; it will also go a long way towards keeping him in fit condition.

Loneliness is irksome to a healthy cocker; his mind needs feeding as well as his body. A happy dog is a fit dog.

Do not expect your dog to obey you before he is thoroughly trained and knows what is expected of him.

Lastly, keep an eye on your dog's general condition. A dry nose, staring coat, running eyes or lassitude, are sure signs of something wrong.

CHAPTER V

For the benefit of those who are new to cockers and have not been fortunate enough to see the certificate winners of recent times, I will give brief descriptions.

In blues we have Mr. H. S. Lloyd's "wizard" bitch Tracey Witch of Ware, who has had a brilliant show career and won no fewer than fifty Challenge Certificates and twice supreme champion of Cruft's. She is by Falconers Padlock of Ware out of Whist.

Next comes Mrs. Gold's light blue dog, Ch. Oxshott Marxedes, who is home-bred by Falconers Mark of Ware ex Berrazanne of Oxshott. One of the best blues of this decade, who has had a very colourful show record, having won about thirty Challenge Certificates, and is proving a great stud force.

Mr. Braddon's blue roan Champion Blue Flint of Ide is a favourite of many. He is a cockery little dog with a good head and short back; his sire is the great dog Harley Sandylands Flare ex Falconers Fuchsia.

Mr. Lloyd's Sh. Ch. Jowyn Blue Boy of Ware is a most attractively marked blue and is probably one of the best-headed dogs on the bench. A great mover, he is a worthy winner of many certificates. By Fantee Silver Sentinel ex Cartref Charmer.

Sh. Ch. Merryworth Matches, a black and white of the highest order, came out and quickly won her three certificates. She is by Colinwood Firebrand out of Merryworth Magical.

Mr. A. W. Collins bred, owned and exhibited Champion Colinwood Cowboy, a cobby little black white and tan who has become a famous sire. Cowboy won four Challenge Certificates and retired at the zenith of his success. His sire is Blackmoor Brand ex Colinwood Cigarette.

Mrs. Doxford's Sh. Ch. Broomleaf Black and Tan. This little lady was the cause of much criticism when she won her first certificate at the Richmond Show, no doubt due to the fact that she was the first black and tan to win a similar honour for many years past, but she quickly made many friends, and gained further honours, winning three certificates in a short time. She was sired by Champion Broomleaf Bonny Lad of Shillwater out of Butterfly of Broomleaf.

Mr. Page's Sh. Ch. Dellah Pin-up Girl, a lovely orange roan bitch, has a beautiful head free of exaggeration and an exceptional body. She has deservedly won her three certificates. Her sire is Augustus of Wykey ex Dellah Joyful Girl.

Sh. Ch. Sixshot Sugar Bird was supreme cocker champion at Cruft's in 1955. She was also supreme champion in show at The Cocker Club, the two most coveted wins in the cocker world. She is black by Sixshot Willy Wagtail out of Dorswick Love in a Mist, owned by the author.

Mr. Braddon's Champion Rodwood Lass of Sandover. This beautiful tricolour bitch is a joy, and her ring presence cannot be overlooked. I awarded her the bitch certificate at Cheltenham when she was six and a half years of age. I thought she was better than ever before. She is by Falconers Mark of Ware out of Mareway Marie.

Sixshot Black Swan, who figures in most of the solid coloured pedigrees of today, was sired by Treetops Terrific out of Sixshot Brown Owl. Owned by the author.

Mrs. de Casembroots Sh. Ch. Treetops Walkie Talkie, probably one of the best black dogs bred in this Kennel. A short, cobby cockery little dog, he is by Treetops Trader out of Treetops Tiller Girl.

Mrs. Doxford's Broomleaf Torquil of Churdles. A merry moving dog, he possesses a good head and a nice, compact body. His sire is Champion Broomleaf Bonny Lad of Shillwater and his dam Serenade of Traquair.

Sh. Ch. Sixshot Storm Bird has made a great name in the red section; he is by Sixshot Woodywoodpecker out of Sixshot Cuckoo.

Mrs. Robb's Foxbar Sandylands Silk. This beautiful little black bitch took a lot of beating. Sweet in expression and beautifully balanced throughout. By Sixshot Black Swan out of Sandylands Red Sue.

Mrs. Doxford's Ch. Broomleaf Bonny Lad of Shillwater has taken a prominent place in the show world, having had a great run of successes. As he walks into the ring he puts on that "Here I am" air and is difficult to pass over. A sound red dog sired by Blare of Broomleaf out of Caroline of Shillwater.

Sh. Ch. Sixshot Woodywoodpecker. A red dog by Sixshot Willy

Wagtail out of Sixshot Nightingale, at the time of writing has won six Challenge Certificates. Owned by the author.

Mr. Braddon's Golden Rod of Ide. A lovely red dog with perfect balance, one of the greatest assets for a show dog. Sired by Sixshot Black Swan out of Lotusflower of Sorrelsun.

Mrs. Smallwood's Knoleforth Dryad. This glorious red bitch is seldom seen in the show ring but was good enough to win the certificate at the L.K.A. in the keenest competition. It is a great pity we have seen so little of her. She is by Sixshot Willy Wagtail out of Cherry of Bridene.

Mrs. Doxford's Sh. Ch. Broomleaf Primula of Kenavon. It would be difficult to find a red bitch with a better head, neck and shoulder. Her sire is Sixshot Willy Wagtail and her dam Kenavon Bran of Broomleaf.

Mr. Joe Braddon's Golden Rule of Ide is a superbly proportioned dog, with head of the right balance. Rule was a grand dog, but unfortunately died prematurely. He will be remembered as a great show dog and a successful sire. His own sire was Champion Golden Rod of Ide and his dam Ringlands Pin-up Girl.

Mrs. de Casembroot's Treetops Truce. His all-round excellence brought him well to the fore. A famous sire, he is by Treetops Tyrian out of Treetops Tendril.

Mrs. Rothwell's champion Talwrn Riverbank Rainmaker is a blue roan, an exquisite little lady with a short, cobby body and a very important head. I had the pleasure of awarding her the Reserve Certificate at Ayr when she was fourteen months of age. This was her first; after that she won ten Reserve Certificates before winning her first Challenge Certificate. Her sire is Harley Riverbank Recall and her dam is Riverbank Regina.

Miss Mingay's aptly named Sh. Ch. Bonny Lass of Kenavon is the best, as well as the most successful, of this small select Kennel. She well deserved her certificates. A beautiful red bitch. Her sire is Champion Broomleaf Bonny Lad of Shillwater and her dam Bramble of Kenavon.

Mrs. Doxford's Sh. Ch. Broomleaf Ballet Shoes. This red bitch is a real little cocker all through; has a great personality; her vivacity and movement are so cocker-like that it is not surprising she has won consistently. Her sire is Broomleaf Kim of Churdles and her dam Brown Bess of Broomleaf.

Miss Macmillan's Lochranza Lisbon Story. There are few better red bitches; a sweet head, and her neck, shoulder placement, ribs, brisket and general outline are all one could wish for. She is by Treetops Truce out of Lochranza Laughing Imp.

Mr. Bebb's Ronfil Regent is a showy black and white dog. His body is short and compact, whilst his head is clean-cut and well balanced. A worthy certificate winner. Sired by Champion Colinwood Cowboy out of Dream Delight.

Mrs. Jones's Sh. C. Courtdale China Model is appropriately named; sweetest of heads, coupled with a short back; good in ribs and hindquarters; moves as a cocker should; a really outstanding bitch. Her sire is Ronfil Regent and her dam Polly of Halford.

Mr. Bebb's Talwrn Tobacco is a most attractively marked light blue roan and tan, who immediately catches the eye as he walks into the ring. He won his certificate at Bournemouth. His sire is Colinwood Mountie, his dam Sandholme Sequin.

Mr. Collins's Colinwood Roughrider. A black, white and tan; a most handsome home-bred dog of the real Colinwood type. He quickly established a reputation as a stud dog by siring Champion Colinwood Son-of-a-Gun. Roughrider won his certificate at Belfast. His sire is Champion Colinwood Cowboy and his dam Colinwood Dainty.

Mrs. Wylde's Solinda of Traquair. I have never had the pleasure of seeing this great celebrity but I understand she is a very beautiful red bitch, who became famous overnight and caused something of a sensation when she won the certificate and best of breed at Windsor Championship Show in 1952 over many seasoned winners. Her sire is Champion Broomleaf Bonny Lad of Shillwater and her dam Sweet Sue of Traquair. I know Sweet Sue well; she is a grand little lady and a daughter of Sixshot Willy Wagtail.

Mr. Braddon's Domino of Ide. A beautiful home-bred son of two famous parents; his colour is black and white; he owns a lovely head and good outline. His sire is Champion Blue Flash of Ide and his dam the lovely Champion Rodwood Lass of Sandover.

Sixshot Polly The Black Hen, won her junior warrant and the challenge certificate at Leeds before going to Switzerland.

Mr. D. L. and Mrs. M. Page's Dellah Merry Maker of Wykey. This blue dog is a favourite of mine, and I was pleased to award him the certificate at the Cocker Club in 1958. He has a beautiful head well chiselled, fine sloping shoulders and a short deep body. His sire is Joywyn Blue Boy of Ware and his dam Dellah Merry Maid of Wykey.

Mr. Mansfield's Ch. Lucklena Musical Maid. This most attractive little lady is light blue. She is not a big one, but compact and well built with true cocker type. I liked her enough to award her the certificate at the National Birmingham in keen competition. Her sire is Ch. Domino of Ide and her dam Lucklena Melodious Maid.

Mr. Weirs' Sh. Ch. Winter Harvest of Weirdene. This young dark blue dog has had a brilliant show career to date, and in my opinion was the best of his colour out in 1958. He won his first certificate at the early age of eleven months. He is home-bred by Aust Ch. Wingsahore of Weirdene. His dam is the good bitch Weirdene Trech Zenda.

Mrs. Doxford's Sh. Ch. Broomleaf Black-eyed Susan. An outstanding red bitch, her name is inclined to confuse. Possibly one of the best bred in this famous kennel. Her head is sweet and she has a short deep body with wonderful ribs and quarters, her movement is a joy. She won her first certificate, and was Supreme Champion at the Cocker Club Show in 1958. Two more certificates quickly followed. Her sire is Billy Bud of Broomleaf and her dam Bubbley of Broomleaf.

Sh. Ch. Sixshot Shore Lark. This red bitch at the time of going to print has won three challenge certificates and eleven reserve certificates. She is by Sh. Ch. Sixshot Storm Bird out of Sixshot Moorhen, owned by the author.

Mr. Collins's Ch. Colinwood Silver Lariot caused a sensation when he came out to win the certificate and best of breed over many seasoned winners at the age of twenty months. Since then he has gone on to great things, winning fifty-five certificates and many times best in show, at championship shows Lariot has become world-famous and is considered by many the best blue dog ever. His sire is Joywyn Blue Flash; his dam Truslers Misty Morn.

Miss Hahn's Sh. Ch. Valjoker of Misbourne, the young black dog which had so many sensational wins in 1958, is a short cockery little dog, a great showman and as sound as a bell. Sired by Sixshot the Black Cockatoo out of Wendayle Valjolie of Misbourne.

Mrs. Clokes Sh. Ch. Gatehampton Black Sambo of Lochnell, won his junior warrant at an early age and caused a sensation when he won the C.C. at Birmingham, beating many seasoned winners.

Mr. and Mrs. Wise's Sh. Ch. Astrawin Aphrodite, a lovely

black bitch, has all the essentials that make a good cocker and it is not surprising that she has a long list of certificates to her credit. She is sired by Sixshot the Black Cockatoo out of Astrawin Arabesque. Mr. and Mrs. Wise's Sh. Ch. Astrawin April Fire is a delightful red dog, possessing tremendous type and solidity; his sire is Sh. Ch. Lochranza Merryleaf Eigar out of Astrawin April Flame.

Mrs. Doxford's Sh. Ch. Blackbird of Broomleaf is a good dog from every angle; he won his first certificate at Crufts in 1965; sired by Lochranza Merryleaf Eigar out of Sh. Ch. Broomleaf Blackeyed Susan.

Miss Collins' Sh. Ch. Colinwood Jackdaw of Lochnell is a fine example of a dog; he has type, balance and character and quickly became a champion. He was sired by Sh. Ch. Blackbird of Broomleaf ex Lochranza Red Sash of Lochnell.

Mrs. Jones's Sh. Ch. Courtdale Flag Lieutenant, a blue dog is a perfect example of the breed; he has had some great wins, and has sired many beautiful specimens; by Courtdale Colinwood Seahawk ex Courtdale Kinkelbridge Gina.

Mr. Aulds' Sh. Ch. Glencora Black Ace is a worthy champion. A great stud dog, he has a beautiful head and short cobby body; sired by Sixshot the Black Cockatoo, out of Sh. Ch. Black Jade of Lochnell.

Mrs. Camerons' Sh. Ch. Val of Lochnell. I liked this red dog well enough to give him his third certificate at Bath in 1966; sired by Valentine of Lochnell, out of Alexandra of Lochnell.

Mrs. Tosh's Sh. Ch. Lochdene Pepper Pot. I like this red bitch immensely, and was pleased to award her The Certificate at Crufts in 1965; her sire is Sh. Ch. Glencora Black Ace out of Lochdene Bubble Gum.

Mrs. Owne's Sh. Ch. Saffron of Settnor is a beautiful orange roan bitch, and a worthy champion. By Dorna Dambuster, out of Courtdale Blue Willow of Settnor.

Sh. Ch. Sixshot Dan The Duck. This red dog made cocker history be gaining his title at his first three championship shows. Sired by Sh. Ch. Sixshot Storm Bird out of Sixshot Garden Warbler; owned by the author.

Mrs. Woodbridge's Sh. Ch. Quettadene Dream Awhile. A black bitch with a sweet head, and short well ribbed body. She has many admirers; her sire is Sh. Ch. Lochranza Merryleaf Eigar ex Quettadene Prudence.

Mrs. Neilson's Sh. Ch. Noslien Naughty Nineties. This beautiful red bitch is a great favourite and carries her years well. I was pleased to award her another certificate at Birmingham in 1966 at the age of six years; sired by Sh. Ch. Lochranza Dancing Master out of Noslien Nainsook.

Miss Macmillan's Sh. Ch. Lochranza Merryleaf Eigar left his mark on the breed, before being exported. Many famous winners are sired by this great dog; his sire is Sh. Ch. Lochranza Dancing Master ex Merrleaf Corine.

Sh. Ch. Sixshot Otto The Owl, red son of two famous parents, Sh. Ch. Sixshot Woodywoodpecker ex Sh. Ch. Sixshot Sugar Bird, owned by the author.

Mr. Mansfield's Ch. Lucklena Musical Director won his third certificate at Paignton in 1966, and after that very quickly qualified in the field, becoming a full champion. He is a beautiful dog and has had many great wins; sired by the one and only Ch. Colinwood Lariot, out of the equally famous Ch. Lucklena Musical Maid.

Mr. Alsop's Sh. Ch. Topbrands Blue Prince is a dazzling black and white, always shown in superb condition. He has a beautiful head, and great substance; his sire is Friesian Lad out of Topbrands Sylvaqueen.

Mrs. Caddy's Sh. Ch. Quaine Parrandero's all round excellence has enabled him to qualify for his title. He owns an exceptionally good head free of exaggeration; his sire is Ch. Colinwood Silver Lariot ex Quaine Pandora.

CHAPTER VI

Cockers of the United States of America. America's Cocker. The Cocker Spaniel in New Zealand.

COCKERS OF THE UNITED STATES OF AMERICA
WITH THE KIND HELP OF
JUDGE TOWNSEND SCUDDER

THERE is authority, supported by reliable evidence, for stating that before the arrival in America of the English the native Indians had domesticated the dog. In November 1620, Colonial Governor Bradford writes that Captain Miles Standish on Cape Cod met a party of Indians with a dog, and in *Mason's Pequot War* it is recorded that in 1637 an Indian dog gave warning of the imminence of the English attack on Pequot Fort. As to the first "spaniel" in America, that spaniel can boast of sharing the cherished pride of many an American—of having had as ancestor a passenger on the *Mayflower*.

Howard M. Chapin in his brochure *Dogs in Early New England* informs us that the *Mayflower* on her famous voyage in 1620 brought two dogs, a mastiff and a spaniel, to New England. The two dogs were permanent settlers. In *Mourt's Relation*, 1622, pp. 27, 28 and 29, are recited some of the hardships suffered by these four-footed pilgrims. It is told how one John Goodman and one Peter Browne, having a great mastiff bitch with them and a "Spannell", "They found a great Deare, the dogs chased him and they followed so far as they lost themselves . . ." Under the date of January 19th, 1620-21, Mourt tells us:

> "This day John Goodman went abroad . . . having a little spannell with him . . . two great wolves ran after the dog, the dog ran to him and betwixt his leggs for succor . . . he . . . tooke up a sticke and threw at one of them and hit him, and they presently ran both away. . . ."

In what is here quoted we have what well may be evidence of the advent in America of the first spaniel to reach its shores. That was very long ago, but the spaniel is still first dog in America

103

and first dog in their hearts. This story tells us that the *Mayflower* "Spannell" was "a little Spannell". Little spaniels were cocking spaniels or cocker spaniels. May not John Goodman's "Little Spannell" have been the first Cocker Spaniel? John's "Little Spannell" played half that breed's game; he flushed the "great Deare" and "chased him" even if he did omit to retrieve him. "Little Spannell" was excited and tired and he got lost. He had been long at sea. Allowance must be made for all these handicaps on that day.

America's Cocker

The "Cocker Spaniel" of America's favour and pride is an American-made breed of dog derived from an admixture of the blood of various varieties and strains of dogs with "Spaniel" background. From this medley, jumble and mixture of bloods the founders of the American Spaniel Club sought to evolve and develop a breed of sporting spaniel designed and destined to be the smallest of the bird gundogs, of uniform type and conformation, possessed of typical spaniel beauty, intelligence and adaptability, also of deep affection and loyalty; a sporting dog to be equally good as house pet or in the field and, to crown all, to be of colourings and markings to satisfy good taste everywhere. It had to be a dog with love, understanding and intelligence ever showing in his eyes, thoroughly well balanced bodily, and beautiful. A laudable ambition, this. Let us turn to their task of realizing it.

Back in the eighteen seventies, and extending into the eighties, there were in some numbers small, leg-feathered, liver and also reddish-coloured curly coated dogs in both the United States and Canada, commonly called Water Spaniels, Cocker or Cocking Spaniels. They were used extensively by gunners, especially along saltwater fronts, to retrieve wild duck and other aquatic game birds. At this work these dogs were unsurpassed. Also in those times, from England and extensively through Canada, liver-coloured and liver and white spaniels were coming into the United States, as also were black field spaniels. The smaller specimens of these spaniels were also called "cockers" or "cocking spaniels", names descriptive of the sport uses to which these small dogs were commonly put in England, namely,

flushing woodcock and other game birds from low-growing brush
or retrieving shot game from thickets too dense for large dogs to
penetrate. While these cocking spaniels were prone to be small
dogs, not so were many of their offspring, some of their puppies
attaining a size not far from that of the average setter of those
days.

It was from this miscellaneous assortment of dogs of some
spaniel blood that the American spaniel fanciers had to select
foundation stock with which to create the cocker spaniel breed
of their dreams. It was a costly job covering years of research and
intelligent planning. Fortuitous circumstances resulted in the
cocker spaniel becoming a separate breed of dog before standardization. This happy stroke of fortune spurred the members of the
American Spaniel Club to greater efforts worthily to take over,
build up and stabilize this breed. The search for foundation stock
spread all over the country, to Canada, even to England, and
there it was that light dawned. But before it dawned the founders
of the American Spaniel Club and other breeders of "cocking
spaniels" had to learn from sad experience that the registration
of a spaniel in our English Stud Book as a Cocker Spaniel did not
mean that its sire, its dam, or both of them, were registered as
"Cocker Spaniels". They also learned that in England in those
days it was customary, and in order, for breeders of sporting
spaniels to register the puppies of a spaniel litter optionally as of
different strains, varieties or breeds according to the breeder's
estimate of the adaptability of a pup to a particular sporting
use, and this without regard to the pup's background or ancestry,
whether registered or not. To illustrate Champion OBO, the
English ancestor of the American cocker, was the offspring of a
Sussex sire and a Field Spaniel dam, yet eligible for our English
Stud Book registry as a cocker spaniel. As Judge Townsend Scudder points out, the uncertainties, disappointments and confusion
often resulting from breeding to English registered cocker spaniels
were due in part to our lack of understanding of the English
system of classifying for Stud Book registration different members
or branches of the big canine family. To some Americans the
atmosphere of the Kennel Club seemed somewhat formal, at
times chilly, even to visitors in search of guidance in tracing the
ancestry of a dog in Kennel Club Stud Book records. But that
was long, long ago! At that time I understood, or thought I
understood (says Judge Scudder), the English system of division

of dogs into named basic varieties and, holding some of these several varieties to be of one and the same breed for inter-breeding purposes, of authorizing the puppies of such matings to be severally registerable as "Sporting Spaniels" of the variety specified by the registrants. Disappointing throw-back surprises in litters soon taught Americans that English registration of a spaniel as a cocker did not necessarily mean that its parents were cockers, and that the term "cocker" or "cocking spaniel" was often merely descriptive of the work to which a small sporting spaniel might be put in the field. Time measured by years elapsed in America before two types of small spaniels were officially accepted as separate, independent breeds or varieties of breeds of "Sporting Spaniels", under the respective names of "Cocker Spaniels" and "English Cocker Spaniels".

OBO II, AKC No. 4911, sired by Mr. James Farrow's OBO and out of Chloe II, a Bullock bred bitch, was exported from England *in utere* by Mr. F. F. Pitcher and sold to Mr. J. P. Willey. Of OBO II Mr. Watson writes: "OBO II is a nice, compactly built little fellow. His head is a little strong but it is nicely carried; his coat is dense and flat and his legs and feet first class."

Mr. Mason, writing of OBO II in *Our Prize Dogs*, says:

"Skull showing slight coarseness. Muzzle should be deeper with a cleaner cut appearance in every direction; it is wider than we like and the lower incisors project slightly. Ears covered in size, shape, position, quality and carriage. Eye good in colour, size and expression. Neck somewhat too heavy. Chest deep with ribs beautifully sprung. Shoulders strong and free. Back firm. Loin compact and strong. Hindquarters of exquisite formation. Forelegs showing great strength and set into good feet. Stern well set. Carriage gay. Coat showing slight curliness, especially on neck and hindquarters. Feather profuse. A thick-set and sturdy little dog that looks exactly what he is—the prince of stud dogs."

Mr. James Watson writes in *The Dog Book*, "OBO II was always considered a small dog, and he weighed twenty-two and one half pounds." Mr. Mason records him as an even twenty-three pounds. OBO II is said to have been slightly smaller than his sire, English Champion OBO. The latter's measurements are given by Mr. Dalziel in his *British Dogs* (1887): "Weight, 22 lb., height 10 in., length of nose to eye, $2\frac{1}{4}$ in., length of nose to occiput $7\frac{1}{2}$ in., length of nose to set-on of tail 29 in." It is said with seeming justification that English OBO's parents were a Sussex and a field spaniel. The quest for worthy bitches to breed to studs of the OBO line was pursued ardently all over the country, was extended to Canada and even crossed the Atlantic. In those times the cocker spaniel commonly found on the American side of the ocean was badly put together, was out of balance and crooked fronts predominated. Its great assets were its keen hunting instinct, its sweet temperament, the beauty of its expression, the love and devotion which shone in its eyes. Sponsors of the breed who could afford Kennel managers sent them scurrying throughout both the United States and Canada in search of small, sound spaniel bitches possessed of those "somethings" essential in a good sporting dog. There were few thus endowed to be found; as Mr. James Watson writes, "Spaniels up to that period were a motley lot in this country." But already matings of Canadian spaniel bitches to OBO II and to some of his sons were producing promising puppies, and by this time Champion OBO II had been accepted by the American fancy as its "Model Cocker". Thus was laid the foundation of the American cocker. It seems appropriate at this point to note that by 1920 there did not seem to be any consistently winning cocker in America which did not have OBO II blood coursing through his veins. Justly the honour was owing to OBO II to be acclaimed the Founding Father of the Cocker Spaniel breed.

In a letter I received from Judge Townsend Scudder he states:

"I was showing dogs when American Champion OBO won his championship in the Westminster Kennel Show in New York. So far as I know, I seem to be the sole survivor of those who saw him in the flesh on that occasion."

In a further letter he writes:

"It seems fairly probable that the majority of the cockers winning in the shows in America at the present time are descendants of one or more of these four great sons of Robinhurst Foreglow, namely Red Brucie, Midriff Miracle Man, Sandspring Surmise and Limestone Laddie.

I always regretted that I was not the breeder of Foreglow. I acquired him as a very young puppy. To own his sire I purchased the entire Blackstone Kennels of over thirty grown dogs and a few very small puppies to go with them. This purchase seemed to me necessary as the owner of the Blackstone Kennels, forced to give up the Kennels due to Town ordinances prohibiting Kennels in his home town, had to dispose of his Kennels but had decided to keep Blackstone Chief as a pet. Chief was the one dog I wanted. The owner of the Kennels then told me that if I would buy all the dogs of the Kennel at his price he would let 'Chief' go too, and this I did. So it was that I acquired the puppy Foreglow and, as he developed, realized how worth-while he was. Foreglow weighed about twenty-eight pounds and was open to challenge in the U.S.A. The result was that I showed him only a couple of times, as I remember it, but because of his type, soundness, spirit and great beauty, I gave stud service free to those who saw possibilities in Foreglow. They were surprisingly few in those days, just because of the four pounds over-weight, and the dog being short-coupled, up-standing, with a beautifully chiselled skull, square lip and dark eyes well set."

In a letter from Mr. Arthur Frederick Jones, Managing Editor of the *American Kennel Gazette*, he says, "The Hon. Townsend Scudder is not only one of the oldest, but most respected authority on the breed in the United States."

The influence of Red Brucie, the famous sire owned by the late Herman Mellenthin, played a dominant part in the breed a score of years ago, and the progeny of Red Brucie were scattered throughout the fancy. Some figure that the influence was less desirable than it seemed at the time. Red Brucie was born in 1921 and was sired by Robinhurst Foreglow ex Rees Dolly. Red Brucie sired thirty-four champions, and was still producing puppies right up until the time of his death, at the age of fifteen years. He was also the grandsire of American bred Robinhurst of Ware, who was bred by Judge Townsend Scudder, and imported to this country by Mr. H. S. Lloyd. Robinhurst of Ware did a great deal towards establishing our English red cocker.

F. W. Simms

Ch. Colinwood Silver Lariot

Sport and General

A good delivery. Pinehawk Hobo retrieving
to James Wylie

Sport and General

The object achieved. A small Cocker
retrieving a hen pheasant

Sport and General

Typical scene at a Spaniel Field Trial

The Cocker Spaniel in New Zealand

Little was known of the cocker spaniel in New Zealand before 1919. Mr. Leversidge, of the Papanui Kennels, was one of the original breeders. Another well-known breeder and noted judge is Dr. McKillop, of the Praival Kennels, who imported to New Zealand Felbrigg Joe and Fifenella of Ware by Champion Invader of Ware. Since 1939 many good dogs and bitches have been exported from Great Britain and the standard has improved very considerably; heads have become finer and coats are a better texture and less wavy. Dr. Hampton's importation into the islands of Champion Sea Spray of Ware, purchased from Mr. H. S. Lloyd and bred by Mrs. Garrington of the Ulwell Kennels, has greatly helped to improve the breed. In one litter he sired Champion Glendale Rosalind, Champion Glendale Rosella, Champion Glendale Jerrold and Glendale Surprise. This famous litter was bred by Mr. Lightfoot, who owns one of the most powerful Kennels in Australasia; his bitch line was founded from an imported bitch from Australia, who was a grand-daughter of Bazel Otto. Mr. Lightfoot has also imported from England Bugle Boy of Alderstone and Pentavy Tempo of Tanystock. Other good dogs helping to keep the flag flying are Champion Jupiter of Seabury, Champion Branded of Ware, Champion Glendale Serenade, Champion Te Reinga Mitti Max. This is mentioning only a few of the famous dogs. It would be difficult to say which is the best dog in New Zealand today, as the shows are as much as a thousand miles apart. Dogs do not compete against each other in the show ring to the same extent as they do in England.

The following is an extract from the *New Zealand Dog World*:

"New Zealand boasts quite a number of very fine cockers, but there are still too many breeders untroubled about coat. The idea seems to be that if nature doesn't regulate an absence of wave or curl the clippers will. Three weeks before a show, out come the clippers. I have seen electric horse clippers used on a cocker in this country—the razor, the Duplex stripper, the hacksaw blade! The three-weeks-before-a-show folk are those who know what they are about. The hair will grow out for the show and disguise the trimming,

H

is their comfortable reflection. They sniff at the tyros who do their razoring the night before the dog is crated. You've all seen cockers come into the ring with fresh jail-bird cuts, head, ear-junction, back of neck. What they look like! The prevailing dictum abroad seems to be that trimming is all right if you can't see it. I still think it is better if possible to breed dogs that don't need mutilation. If some breeders can achieve this so can others, if they will but take the trouble to breed out blackberry-hedge coats and introduce the flat, and persevere as, for example, Jim Lightfoot has done. Then they would be spared the sight that many cockers present about six weeks after a show and onwards. We all know what the clipped, shorn, razored dogs look like after a show, when the hair starts to grow out. Ideally, there should be no interference with a cocker's coat other than by thumb and forefinger, a general tidying up. If he's bred right he should need little more. Perhaps a little sandpaper—that leaves no ugly cuts and ridges, provokes no woolly aftergrowth. Please don't take that to mean that I think cockers should be put down like woolly lambs or hairy goats. I detest them so. I would have them as the standard requires, but sleek and smooth from the operation of inherited characteristics, not the horse clippers."

CHAPTER VII

The Cocker Spaniel as a Gundog

By P. R. A. Moxon

Early training. Sitting to command. Dropping at a distance. Steadiness to thrown dummy. Dropping to shot. Working in water. Introduction to game. Questing for game and steadiness. First shooting experience. General suggestions.

THE training of cocker spaniels for the gun differs in no wise from that of other spaniels, except insofar as the cocker is inclined to be an individualist and requires greater firmness and tact in handling. When properly trained a cocker of working strain is one of the most useful dogs that a rough shooter can have, being keen, fearless in cover and water, and possessing a good nose for both fur and feather. In regard to retrieving, this varies from dog to dog, but some of the best retrieving gundogs I have seen have been cockers. With experience these little dogs can deal with any game, including cock pheasants and even hares.

The king-pin of gundog training is OBEDIENCE. A dog which is not obedient is not trained, no matter how brilliant a gamefinder it may be. A wild, unruly gundog of any breed is a curse to the shooter rather than a blessing, putting up game out of range of the gun and generally spoiling sport for everyone present. Wild dogs may develop wonderful noses and find plenty of game, it is true, but they spoil more sport than they provide, and this is particularly true of wild spaniels. The cocker is inclined to be wilful and therefore needs special attention paid to its preliminary "hand" or obedience training. The trainer must be firm but kind, and very patient. The old saw about "a woman, a spaniel and a walnut tree, the more you beat them the better they be" may be true about women and walnut trees—I don't pretend to know—but as far as cocker spaniels are concerned the less punishment that is given the better. This is not to say that punishment has to be altogether dispensed with, but I wish to dispel the illusion, still retained in some quarters, that "the stick" is the only method whereby cockers can be trained. Punishment handed out indiscriminately and without showing the dog where it is at fault can produce only two types of gundog—the cowed cringing wretch that is the pity of all who behold it, or the hardened

III

sinner who will please himself and accept a beating as a matter of course. No thinking man desires to own either type of spaniel.

What is required of a cocker spaniel in the field? Normally, the cocker is used to quest within gunshot for unshot game, flush it and retrieve the slain only upon command. It must remain steady when rabbits bolt or game gets on the wing, and is generally taught to drop both to flush and shot. There are some owners who not only use their cockers thus but also like them to act as retrievers pure and simple when game is being driven. To use a cocker in this manner, whilst by no means impossible, is asking a lot of a breed whose natural instinct is to be on the move the whole time. I have found that whilst certain individuals will take kindly to the idea of waiting in a butt or at a pheasant stand for driven game, the majority of cockers are far too restless and are inclined to become over-excited, whine and even yap when the birds come over and the guns start firing. Such dogs are a nuisance to both handler and to the other guns present, and generally end up by being tethered to their masters' sides if not removed from the shooting field altogether. My advice to cocker owners is, therefore, not to expect too much from the breed in this respect, but to use the dogs mainly, if not solely, for their natural work as questing dogs when game is walked up, plus, of course, retrieving when required.

EARLY TRAINING

Training to come to call, to retrieve a small dummy, and to quest light cover can begin at a very early age—almost from the nest stage, in fact. The puppy should be taught its name and to come in to a particular whistle (I use two quick toots on a high-pitched staghorn whistle for this), and this is best accomplished by repeating the name, followed by the whistle signal, and the giving of an edible reward. This creates an association between name and whistle and something pleasant, and to puppies, like children, nothing is more pleasant than something to eat! Let the puppy run about on the lawn and suddenly call his name and give your whistle signal, and immediately he comes in make much of him. In cases of stubbornness run up to and past the puppy, repeating name and whistle, and in a very short time you will have a puppy obedient to call.

Retrieving a small dummy (which can be a ball, an old glove rolled up or a small, stuffed rabbit skin) can be commenced as soon as the above lesson has been learned. Most worth-while cockers have a natural retrieving instinct and if you throw your dummy a short way on bare ground even the youngest puppy will usually run after it and pick it up. Immediately this happens call and whistle him in and praise him, but do not snatch the retrieve away at once. Take it very gently and use only slight pressure on the lips if there is a tendency for the pupil to hang on. If a puppy seems to prefer running off with the dummy to his kennel or basket, place yourself in a position where you can intercept him on the inward journey, and adopt the same procedure. Encourage the puppy to come right up to you and stand with the dummy in his mouth in front of you. If you try to remove it too quickly he may get into the habit of circling round you, which must at all costs be avoided. A good, clean delivery is essential in a well-trained gundog.

At first the puppy can be allowed to run-in and pick up the dummy immediately it is thrown, but ultimately he must wait on the drop until you give the command to fetch. This cannot be taught until the puppy has learned to sit to command, which is the next important step in training, and for this reason dummy practice must not be overdone, but carried out only sufficiently often to retain keenness and a willing return and delivery. As the puppy grows older, however, you can and should vary the practice by throwing the dummy into cover of gradually increasing degrees of thickness, rough grass, cabbages, light bracken, etc., to encourage the hunting instinct, love of cover and use of nose.

By the time the average puppy is five or six months old it should be sufficiently bold to withstand serious obedience training, the first stage of which is sitting to command. Individuals vary, of course, and as I point out in a book I recently published no hard and fast rule about age can be laid down. Bold puppies can be started earlier than shy ones, and really nervy dogs are best left until they are eight or nine months of age. In any event you should do everything you can to instil confidence and courage by taking the puppy about and letting it meet people and things —become generally world-wise, in other words. This will never occur if the puppy is kept rigidly in kennel between lessons, although of course you must not go to the other extreme and allow all and sundry to handle and fool about with the puppy.

Common sense should dictate how much licence can be allowed in this respect.

SITTING TO COMMAND

Teaching a puppy to sit to command is most important and must be done very thoroughly. I try to teach my pupils to drop to the word "Hup!", to a *single, long* blast on the whistle and to the raised hand. Spaniels should also drop to shot, and I am assuming that you have already accustomed yours to the sound of gunfire so that it is neither gunshy nor gun-nervy. Firing a gun at feeding-time at gradually decreasing distances from the kennel or house is probably the best way of getting a puppy used to gunfire. Once sitting to command has been learned by the pupil, the report of the gun must also be made to signify an immediate drop.

A leather slip lead is useful for early training—one which has a loop at one end for your hand and a ring through which the lead can be passed to form a running noose at the other. The noose is slipped over the puppy's head and he is gradually taught to walk without lagging behind or pulling ahead by manipulation of the lead. Jerk the lead sharply and give the erring pupil an "electric shock". Usually there is a certain amount of reluctance to behave on the lead at first but puppies can be gradually accustomed to wearing collar and lead from an early age. This will be helpful when serious training starts.

To teach the drop, have your puppy walking on the slip lead at your left side, preferably on the lawn or in a field away from all distractions. Walk the puppy along, stop suddenly, raise your right hand and give the previously decided command to drop. The puppy does not understand what you require, so show him by pressing him firmly down on his haunches with the left hand whilst holding the lead tight with the right. Gradually straighten your back and stand still. If the puppy moves, manipulate the lead to force him back into a sitting position, repeating the command sharply. Keep him thus for a few moments, then pat him and walk on, repeating the procedure over and over again for ten minutes or so. Training lessons should always be short in the early days—ten to fifteen minutes being plenty long enough, otherwise the pupil is apt to become bored and dispirited. It is far better to give two or even three short spells of training per day than one over-long lesson. A bored puppy will never learn properly and will prove a real problem to deal with.

If your puppy takes to his dropping lessons and quickly gets the hang of them you need not give an edible reward each time he drops, but a difficult or reluctant puppy can be encouraged in this way if it really seems necessary. Bribery is best dispensed with altogether if possible and if used should never be carried on for too long. A puppy appreciates a pat and a word of praise, however, and I make a point of showing my approval in this way every time the pupil does well. The next step in training is to get the puppy to remain on the drop until given the command to move. This can be commenced as soon as he has thoroughly learned to drop quickly to command and to the whistle, if used— if not, it can be introduced at once by being blown immediately after the vocal command. In a very short while a puppy will respond to the whistle without any spoken command at all, and the voice is "kept in reserve", as it were. The lead is dispensed with as progress advances.

By backing away slowly from the seated puppy you will soon discover whether he is of the restless type or not. Most pups very naturally try to follow their handler the moment he moves away, and now your patience is going to be truly tested. If, when you back away, the puppy moves, repeat the command to drop and reseat him in his original position by taking him by the slack skin under the throat. This must be done *every time he moves*, without exception. Some people "peg down" their pupils with a short chain and peg, thus forcibly restraining the puppy from moving when they back away. This is quite in order in the case of a very stubborn, wilful puppy, but I prefer to do without mechanical aids as far as possible, except the lead in early lessons. However, more of this anon. As soon as the puppy seems to have the right idea, try walking away instead of backing. This will lead to more trouble between you and your pupil, in all probability, but with patience and perseverance on your part you should be able to walk away and leave him on the drop quite happily after a few lessons. If you reseat the puppy every time he makes a move from the very beginning you will quickly establish your mastery over him. Omit to do so once or twice and he will be encouraged to repeat the offence. Never allow a pupil to get the better of you if it can possibly be avoided, or he will tend to lose respect for you and the bond between handler and dog, so necessary for complete success, will be weakened. Cocker spaniels are restless animals by nature and most trainers experience rather more difficulty in obtaining discipline from this breed than from some of the other gundogs.

DROPPING AT A DISTANCE

Once your puppy will drop to command promptly and remain on the drop whilst you walk away, and even hide out of sight, you can teach him to drop at a distance. In some cases it will be found that the pupil sits to command and/or whistle even when at a distance from his handler, simply because you have so thoroughly taught association of ideas between command and the action of dropping. Where special lessons are required, the following method of teaching to drop at a distance will be found very efficient and quick. Simply seat your pupil, walk away about fifteen or twenty yards and whistle him up. Immediately he gets within a few feet of you give the command (vocal or whistle) to drop. Success being achieved, walk on again, repeat the process but each time give the order to sit a little sooner, so that ultimately the puppy will go down instantly at any point between his original position and yourself. Thereafter let him run about in front of you and practise him at dropping wherever he may be in relation to yourself. In some cases it may be found necessary to use a check cord to instil obedience at a distance. This is a cord about ten to fifteen yards long with a ring at one end to make a noose for the pup's head. A few knots are tied in the cord (sash cord does very well) and the dog is made to wear it. When the command to drop is given you stand sharply on the cord, thus bringing the pupil up with a jerk. This same cord can be used to restrain a puppy from running home (as some will) when the first obedience lessons are given.

STEADINESS TO THROWN DUMMY

From this point on your puppy should never be allowed to run-in again to the thrown dummy. At first let him wear a short lead or cord and drop him beside you, holding the lead under your foot. Throw the dummy out and restrain the puppy for half a minute or more before allowing him out to retrieve,

Sh. Ch. Golden Star of Ulwell

Sh. Ch. Crosbeian Thornfalcon Flamenco

Ch. Highomar Hallelajah, U.S.A.

Sh. Ch. Val of Lochnell

commanding him to sit should he stand up and struggle to go after the dummy, as he almost certainly will. Continue the exercise until you can safely dispense with the lead, but always be on the alert and position yourself so that you can intercept the puppy should he attempt to run-in to the thrown dummy. Keep him on the drop for an appreciable time before sending him out to retrieve, and always despatch him with the same command: "Fetch it!", "Hi, lost!", "Seek!", or what you will. Readers may consider that I have used up a lot of space in dealing with preliminary obedience. I can assure them from personal experience that this is no waste, for half the battle in dog training is won if the initial work is thoroughly carried out. Field work on game will come naturally to a good cocker, but it will be useless unless you have got the dog under control and working for *you* instead of for himself.

DROPPING TO SHOT. RETRIEVING PRACTICE

Your puppy must now be taught to drop to shot. Using a blank-cartridge pistol or a shotgun, you simply give a sharp command to drop and immediately throw up the gun and fire. In a very short while the shot acts as another signal to drop, although later on when the "real thing" is being hunted you will probably find your pupil stands rather than drops to shot. Providing no movement is made this is all right, but insisting upon a complete drop is better. Naturally, no puppy should receive these gunfire lessons until he is completely confident and unafraid of the report. Further steadiness practice can be given by throwing the dummy into cover of gradually increasing degrees of thickness and firing the gun whilst the dummy is in the air, thus simulating real shooting conditions. The pupil is despatched to retrieve after a wait on the drop, and as progress is made so the retrieves can be made more difficult by being made longer and longer and the cover more formidable. *Always whistle up* the pupil at the moment his head goes down to pick up. Artificial drag lines can be laid with the dummy at this juncture, thus giving the pupil a "line" to follow as he will later have in the field when sent for wounded birds. The line should be laid upwind at first, out of sight of the pupil and without yourself fouling the scent. This can be accomplished by using a long pole, or fishing rod and line, with the dummy attached and held as far from you as possible, or by getting an assistant to hold the other end of a long rope, to the centre of which the dummy has been tied. Later on, when experience has been gained, dead birds and rabbits can be used in just the same way.

Advanced retrieving practice can be given with the dummy as soon as a puppy is really obedient. This includes dropping the pupil and walking out yourself to throw the dummy, and the ever-useful "going back" lesson. Drop the dummy in full sight of the puppy, walk him on and send him back over ever-increasing distances for it. As this is learned, do not let him see the dummy fall—send him out on a "blind retrieve" for it. Whistle immediately he picks up. In the shooting field he will often be called upon to look for game which he did not see fall. This lesson will also encourage use of nose and a speedy return. If you wish to put a real "finish" upon your pupil, utilize this lesson for dropping him on the way out to his retrieve, using a check cord if necessary. This lesson, tactully conducted, will get him under even better control and may well come in useful if ever you run in Trials and you see the dog making for the wrong bird. A dog which can be stopped and redirected on a retrieve is well on the way to becoming trained. Use clear-cut hand signals to help your pupil wherever possible, especially for indicating the direction of a retrieve. Encourage a love of cover and let the dog quest it freely, trying at first to find game-free cover until steadiness work has been given.

Working in Water. Jumping Fences and Gates

Any retrieving gundog worthy of the name must face water and retrieve therefrom. Most cockers of working strain take to water very quickly and love working in it. Introduction to it should be made on a warm day and force should not be used. Choose a pond or stream with gently shelving banks and throw a ball or dummy a little way in. If this does not work throw in something eatable, or make use of a trained and keen water dog as an example. Wade in and paddle about yourself if you feel inclined—anything to encourage the puppy and promote confidence in water. Once he will swim a little way encourage him farther and farther out until you can see that he really has the idea. Then teach him to go across water and climb the opposite bank to seek the dummy. Tact and perseverance on your part are almost sure to be successful—completely water-shy cockers are a rarity—but you must be gentle and patient.

Jumping fences and gates is taught quite easily once a puppy is well grown and confident. Just take him for walks and climb easy fences yourself and walk on. If there are no suitable, easy places nearby it is worth while constructing a jump and bribing the puppy over it either with the dummy or with food, or allow an experienced dog to set an example. Do not let the first places be too difficult, of course, and avoid barbed wire and fences which are not fairly solid to start with. Confidence must be created—once you have your puppy jumping for the love of it you will have no more trouble. All that remains to be done is to practice retrieving over jumps of different kinds.

INTRODUCTION TO GAME

Up to this point all training has been conducted artificially, using a dummy for retrieving practice. The dummy has been gradually increased in size and weight so that by the time your pupil is ready to retrieve real game it is of a fair size and weight. The change-over will not therefore strain the neck muscles of a small cocker and cause a poor delivery. The first rabbits and birds used for retrieving practice must be *fresh shot but cold*, and quite free from blood and damage. In the first instance drop the bird in full view of the dog, as you have been doing with the dummy, walk him on and send him back for it. Whistle him up the moment his head goes down to retrieve, and if he hesitates run away as you did in the early lessons. If the puppy refuses to pick up, or starts to play with the bird, take it and throw it like a dummy, running away and calling him up the moment his head goes down to it. Few cockers refuse to retrieve game after a while. Those which do require special treatment which cannot be discussed here owing to lack of space. Common sense should dictate the steps to be taken when difficulties are encountered. Once a puppy is accustomed to picking up cold birds, and does not attempt to play with or bite them, he can be tried with warm game or rabbits in the same way. Always remember to hurry the puppy up by whistling and calling the moment he picks up, so that there is not time for him to think about playing with the game. Scent trail lessons, as previously given with the dummy, can now be carried out with advantage, using dead birds or rabbits. Never use the same specimen for more than one, or at the outside two, retrieves. To use the same bird or rabbit again and again leads to bad delivery, if not refusal to retrieve, and hard mouth.

QUESTING FOR GAME AND STEADINESS

Our cocker spaniel, having been taught obedience and control and to retrieve from cover and water, must now have more advanced tuition in questing for game and remaining steady to it. Spaniels are natural questers and quickly learn to quarter their ground in a systematic manner with very little aid from their handler. Use a separate command for questing—I always snap my fingers and say, "Hi, seek!" for this, starting the pupil off to hunt to one side of me. It is necessary that a spaniel quest within gunshot range, so when the limit of about twenty or twenty-five yards is reached I attract his attention by name or whistle and wave my hand over to encourage him to quest on the other side. All this time I am walking steadily forward and keeping the dog on the move. The puppy which does not quickly "cotton on" to the idea is made to drop by whistle when he reaches the limit of his range to one side, and then waved over. If all else fails, small pieces of biscuit can be thrown out to right and left to encourage the puppy to "weave" about, but previous lessons have usually instructed him to watch your hand movements closely and work to them. If the puppy ranges too far whistle him back with your usual "come back" whistle, and back away yourself. The ideal place for these early questing lessons to be taught in is a smallish meadow of rough grass, light clover or spring wheat —somewhere where the puppy can easily be seen but with enough cover to interest him and make him work. Naturally, though it is an advantage that there should be some scent of game or rabbits in such a place it is to be hoped that actual game will not be present as the pupil has yet to learn to be steady. An accidental flush might ruin chances of future steadiness, so after one or two lessons as suggested above the next step is to introduce him to game, or rather rabbits, and teach strict steadiness.

Most professional trainers use a rabbit pen for this purpose—a specially constructed enclosure of a quarter of an acre or more, containing live rabbits and natural cover. If you can construct such a pen—even a small one containing only one or two rabbits—or have access to one belonging to someone else, a great deal of work and worry will be avoided. Failing this, turning a tame rabbit out on the lawn or in the cabbage patch for a few moments will prove a great help. You will have to adapt your training to whatever system you can evolve with the time and space at your disposal.

When using a rabbit pen, introduce the puppy into it on a lead or check cord. Walk him round until you find a rabbit, and immediately the latter bolts give the command to drop and jerk the puppy down. Carry this on for ten or fifteen minutes, making the pupil drop each time a rabbit bolts, using the voice, whistle and lead to ensure prompt obedience. After a few lessons the puppy will show signs of knowing what is required, and is then worked with the cord trailing, so that if he does break away after bunny you can stop him and make him sit. Punishment should not be given unless absolutely essential, and should be given in such a manner that the dog knows what it is for. Always punish in the act of committing the crime if possible, or at any rate take the puppy back to the exact spot where he did wrong and whip him there. Never, never beat a dog when he returns to you—always take him back to the scene of his crime. Punishing by holding and shaking is usually more effective than a whipping, and afterwards give him a minute or two on the drop to meditate upon his crime.

As soon as the puppy becomes reliable when close to you, let him quest naturally if the pen is large enough, dropping him by voice or whistle should he show signs of chasing. Keep the check cord in reserve for cases of flagrant disobedience. In many instances the pupil does not drop after a time, but simply stands and watches the rabbit away. Insist upon a drop, at any rate to begin with. Take the gun or pistol into the pen at this stage and fire it as the rabbit bolts, thus creating a "natural" situation which will always be occurring in the future. Some cockers will show a tendency to "point" their rabbits—this is to be encouraged; stand stock still when it occurs. Keep the puppy pointing for as long as possible, then walk in and push the rabbit up yourself, making the pupil drop as you do so. If you always allow the dog to push the rabbit out himself he will soon cease to point and flush at once. When a spaniel is questing in the pen and puts up a rabbit make him hunt in a different direction after the rabbit bolts. Never allow him to follow the rabbit. If the pen is large enough, walk down the middle of it, making the puppy range from side to side in front of you and within range. Retrievers and many spaniels are made to retrieve the dummy in the pen from nearby grazing rabbits (some of which are usually tame or semi-tame for this purpose), and this is a further aid to steadiness.

However, in a small pen or on the lawn with only one rabbit, such refinements are not possible, and so you will have to proceed as above on any available field or cover where rabbits can be found in sufficient quantities. It naturally takes longer to steady a puppy on natural ground, but it can be and often is done. Providing the pupil has never been allowed to self-hunt and chase game and rabbits, steadiness is not really difficult to inculcate in any gundog, for by this system of training the puppy is taught right before it learns to do wrong, and obedience is acquired gradually and naturally. Once the puppy shows that he has the right idea on rabbits he can be taken into fields and woods where all types of game will be encountered, made to quest and have shots fired over him. Do not shoot to kill until you are completely sure of his reactions and feel confident of his steadiness.

First Shooting Experience

The first shooting expedition is best undertaken alone or with one friend to shoot whilst you do the handling. Make the puppy quarter the ground and drop to shot and rise of game. Never send him to retrieve if he has shown the slightest sign of unsteadiness and, whilst the early retrieves in the shooting field must be reasonably easy, avoid sending him for birds which lie in the open and can be found by sight alone—this will only encourage unsteadiness. Never send him for birds which show any signs of life until he is proficient at retrieving stone dead ones, and always watch closely and whistle him up the moment his head goes down to pick up. Keep the dog on the drop for fully half a minute, or even longer, after every shot and fall, and despatch to retrieve by command and signal as previously.

As experience is gained on dead birds and rabbits the pupil can be trusted to try for wounded birds or "runners". Avoid putting the dog on to them whilst they are still in sight, and do not be disappointed by early failures or signs of hard mouth. The retrieving of runners is a knack gained only by experience and many young dogs will maul their first few birds and rabbits.

Do all you can to get your dog back to you quickly by *whistling him up the moment he puts his head down to retrieve*, running away from him if necessary. This is why you should always at first try to follow your puppy when out after a retrieve (live or dead) which is in cover but do not, of course, go right up to him. Try to see what is taking place and whistle him up, returning to your original position at the run if necessary. Do not allow your dog to retrieve every bird or rabbit shot—select those which require use of nose and hunting in cover, picking up the easy ones yourself whilst the dog remains on the drop.

Your dog is now well on the way to being trained, and all that is required is further experience. Readers may think that I have made it all seem beautifully easy and have glossed over the snags that are likely to be encountered. If you have the right dog and teach him the right way training *is* easy, but of course many little things arise to trip up the unwary. I cannot go into details nearly as fully as I should wish in a short chapter on training— it is easier to write a book than a chapter on this vast subject!

GENERAL SUGGESTIONS AND ADVICE

As a conclusion I will offer some words of advice which should help the novice handler. Choose your puppy from working parents, preferably those with Field Trial blood in their veins. Commence training to answer name and retrieve a small dummy as early as possible, deferring strict discipline until you know he can "take it". Try to "think like a dog" and, when things go wrong, try to see the situation from the dog's point of view, and apply the remedy at once. Punishment should be given only when really necessary and should be made to fit the crime. It must always be administered at the actual spot where the dog did wrong, or whilst the crime is being committed. Remember that the lessons, though the earlier ones can be intermingled to add variety, must be given in their proper order and that no new lesson should be started until the latest one has been thoroughly mastered by the pupil. Do not make the mistake of hurrying him on to "more interesting work". Plug away at the hand training and obedience until you really have an obedient, steady dog. Give short but frequent spells of training, encourage use of nose and confidence in thick cover and water from the start. Make the change-over from dummy work to the real thing as gradual as possible, and when shooting starts think about your dog rather than your shooting—otherwise you will have wasted a lot of time. When guns go off and game falls, think first of the dog and be ready to prevent him running in or chasing—say "Hup!" or "Sit!" or blow your whistle as a matter of course—always expect the worst, in other words! Then you will not go wrong. Choose your words of command and signals and whistles and stick to them, always using the same one for the same action. Use your hands sensibly to give signals which are clear-cut and definite. Train your puppy away from distractions and other dogs and people. If he seems to be getting bored or restless stop the lesson and put him away for a few hours—a bored puppy does not learn. Be patient but firm at all times, and try to wind up each lesson on a note of success—do not let the pupil "best" you. He must go back to his kennel feeling that you are boss, not that he has won a victory of wills over you.

If you aspire to run your cocker in Field Trials your training should be just the same but, if it is possible, more thorough and prolonged. There are plenty of Stakes run for cocker spaniels only, and nowadays cockers are showing up well in mixed Stakes for any variety of retrieving spaniel. For Trials your dog must be mute, of course—a dog which gives tongue whilst questing is "out" as far as present-day Trials are concerned. You will find that Field Trials are a very enjoyable and sociable type of sport and both you and your dog would benefit from watching and competing. The Field Trial people are a friendly lot and anxious to help newcomers to the game. Quite apart from this, it will be doing cocker spaniels as a breed a great service to train them and enter them at Trials, for they are, after all, *gun*dogs and deserve to be used as such. Spaniels are the shooter's "maid-of-all-work" and cannot be beaten for rough shooting, especially in dense woods and other places where birds and rabbits have to be flushed from thick cover. If you train a dog properly it is a joy to shoot over, and I offer the hope that my few words on the subject will go some way towards restoring the merry little cocker to its rightful place as "the sporting spaniel".

To those who wish to go thoroughly into this absorbing hobby I offer the suggestion that they should read my book, *Gundogs: Training and Field Trials* (Popular Dogs Publishing Co., Ltd.) in which the subject is dealt with comprehensively and in considerable detail.

CHAPTER VIII

SOME COMMONER HEALTH PROBLEMS

By F. Andrew Edgson, MRCVS

Hard-pad or distemper. Disorders of the alimentary tract. Enteritis.
Conditions of the ear. Pyometra or metritis. Interdigital cysts.
Bad breath.

A Cocker Spaniel, like any other dog, can fall foul of various
infections or conditions which may arise from accident or
advancing years. The duty of the owner is to try to protect his or
her charge from these, and today this can be done more effectively
than ever before. The dog born today is indeed fortunate com-
pared with his ancestors of even ten or twenty years ago, and
anybody who has the responsibility of owning a dog and does not
take all the measures available to him to protect his charge is
living in the past, and putting his charge in jeopardy.

A healthy dog is a happy dog and a pleasure to have with
you. If he has, for instance, a dirty mouth or bad ears he will not
only be unhappy but objectionable to have with you. A regular
grooming, and making sure that he is free of parasites are obvious
"musts", but how often do many owners check to make sure that
claws are not too long, not cracked or split, and that the teeth are
free from tartar, and the ears free of wax? These are points which
a spaniel will particularly appreciate with his soft mouth, jowl
and pendulous ears, more than some other less well-endowed
breeds. The very points which make him such a fine specimen do
make him in need of just that little extra attention from time to
time.

In all diseases, protection is better than cure. Even with
modern anti-sera, antibiotics and chemotherapeutics, any disease
is almost always bound to leave behind its damage, however
promptly and effectively the infection is diagnosed, treated and
arrested. This is why, when efficient, modern, vaccines are
available to prevent infections, every advantage should be taken
of them.

The diseases which can kill or harm your dog are as follows:

I   125

"Hard-pad" or "Distemper"

With the progress which veterinary science has made within the past few years, the most important and dangerous infectious disease, "hard-pad", and its closely associated disease, distemper, are both nowadays preventable. It is very much, of course, up to the owner of the dog, or to the dog breeder to take the steps which he can to protect his animals and the breeder or dog owner who today does not vaccinate against at least one disease is as negligent as the mother who does not have her child immunised against diphtheria. Today there is no excuse whatsoever for outbreaks of "hard-pad" or distemper resulting from shows or other doggy occasions. If all dog owners took the simple steps which are readily available to them, "hard-pad" and distemper could become diseases which you only read about in books and never experience in your own particular dog. Anybody who has had the misfortune to have to nurse a dog through "hard-pad" or distemper would say that an effective and active immunisation is an absolute godsend, and yet even today some people do not take this precaution which is easily available to them.

"Hard-pad" and distemper are caused by an ultra-microscopic virus, and the vaccines which are in current use are freeze-dried and are prepared by mixing the culture with a diluent immediately before they are administered to the dog. The virus which is injected, is one which is grown on live cells and as a result produces a good immune response within the animal but without producing the disease in any way. Within the past year another vaccine which has become available is a measles vaccine, and has the added advantage of being able to be used in very young puppies or in dogs which have actually been in contact with infection. This vaccine is of benefit by virtue of the fact that the measles virus is very similar in its type and pathegonicity so far as tissue cells are concerned, to the distemper virus, but again, like the distemper vaccine is incapable of producing the actual clinical disease within the dog. However, with the measles vaccine, when it is injected it does have the effect of occupying the cells which would otherwise be attacked by the "hard-pad" or distemper virus and should the animal come in contact with distemper during the period of protection by the measles vaccine, then the animal will be able to resist the distemper virus. The main advantage of the measles vaccine is that, unlike the ordinary distemper immunising process, the animal is resistant to distemper within a few hours of it being injected. The advantage of this is that it can be used in very young puppies which are at risk, or in dogs which are not immunised with the true distemper vaccine, and which have been in contact with a recent infection. However, it is important to bear in mind that the true distemper vaccines should always be used in animals which are of a mature age, that is ten to twelve weeks of age, as this vaccine will ultimately give a longer time of protection against the condition.

So far as re-vaccination is concerned, it would seem to be highly desirable to boost the immunity which is conveyed by the distemper vaccines at regular intervals, as lack of contact with actual infection may allow the resistance within the animal body to wane and therefore if re-vaccination is not carried out the degree of immunity after several years may not be sufficiently strong to resist a virulent natural strain of the virus.

Nowadays combined vaccines immunising not only against "hard-pad" and distemper but also against the fox encephalitis virus (H.C.C.) or Rubarth's disease, a virus disease which attacks liver tissue, are available. Rubarth's disease is an infection of particular importance to the young or very young puppy and in some instances can produce the "fading" of puppies syndrome.

Other diseases aaginst which vaccination is to be recommended are the two leptospiral diseases of dogs—leptospira icterohaemorrhagiae, and leptospira canicola, the former being rat-borne and an organism which attacks the liver tissues and the latter being carried by dogs and producing severe or chronic kidney damage of an acute or chronic type. Today it is possible to immunise against several of these diseases in two or three combinations, thereby reducing the number of injections that each puppy will require in order to become immunized. These are points, however, which are best discussed with your veterinary surgeon and his advice should be sought when the dog is very young, in order that any vaccination procedures can be done at the right time.

DISORDERS OF THE ALIMENTARY TRACT

The symptoms which are seen in cases of these disorders are commonly shown by vomiting with or without diarrhoea, or constipation.

A dietary indiscretion may be the cause of vomiting and after the offending food has been ejected the dog is frequently perfectly all right again. In all cases of vomiting, however, where this symptom persists the cause should be ascertained, as it may be of a serious nature. In the puppy, in particular, foreign objects such as buttons, stones, needles, bones, may be swallowed and these can produce trouble either in the stomach itself or in the lower parts of the gut such as the small intestine or colon. If you suspect that your dog has swallowed some foreign object, the most important thing is to not give any laxative or purgative such as liquid paraffin or castor oil, and to consult your veterinary surgeon, who may wish to examine him by special procedures such as X-rays, to ascertain if your suspicions are correct and whether or not an operation is indicated. In all cases of vomiting the dog should not be allowed water, although a little barley water or milk and water (half milk, half water) may be given.

In any case of vomiting the dog should not be allowed to have any further food until he has been examined by a veterinary surgeon. In elderly dogs a chronic degenerative nephritis is a common cause of vomiting and this is due to the animal's kidneys being unable to excrete in the urine all the waste products which should be eliminated in this fashion. Again pyometra an infection of the uterus, which is not uncommon in the virgin bitch after the age of five or six years, is again accompanied by an increase in thirst and vomiting. It will be seen therefore that vomiting is not always a straightforward condition such as an upset "tummy".

In puppies worms will cause the symptoms of vomiting and diarrhoea and a worm may sometimes be seen in the vomit or in excreta. Before dosing this type of case for worms the gastritis should be settled down by a careful milk and fish diet for a few days and a little raw white of egg beaten in a quarter of a pint of milk is a useful bland feed in such instances.

ENTERITIS

This is symptomized by loose motions or diarrhoea and occasionally if a gastro-enteritis is present, vomiting also may be seen. The cause is almost invariably a dietary indiscretion which has either produced a direct inflammation of the small and large intestines or which contained harmful bacteria that have produced the inflammation. Today there are many effective remedies that can be prescribed for such cases and your veterinary surgeon will be able to advise and treat the case accordingly. However, supportive treatment in the way of careful feeding is important and arrow-root cooked and mixed with boiled fish or boiled egg makes a good, if rather uninteresting, convalescent diet and this should be continued until the diarrhoea has ceased A periodic diarrhoea in older dogs is sometimes not a simple matter. It may be due to parasites such as tapeworms or other intestinal invaders but occasionally one comes across the animal, just as in humans, who cannot digest adequately certain factors in his diet. Fat, for instance, is not completely digested by some dogs but tests which can be carried out by your veterinary surgeon will elucidate such more complicated cases.

In all cases of abdominal pain it is as well to consult your veterinary surgeon as foreign bodies can, having negotiated the stomach, become lodged in the small intestine. Again diarrhoea may be a constant or intermittent symptom with such foreign bodies or the cause of abdominal pain may be due to bacterial infection which again can be treated effectively.

Conditions of the Ear

The Cocker Spaniel, by virtue of his pendulous ears, is perhaps more prone to conditions of the ear than other breeds. When an ear is affected, the dog holds its head on one side, shakes its head or scratches at the offending ear. The cause may be quite simple such as a little natural secretion may have accumulated and caused a local irritation but there may be an inflammation of the outer ear canal, this condition frequently being referred to by breeders as "canker". However, a foreign body may have got into the external meatus of the ear and this will have to be removed by your veterinary surgeon using a local or general anaesthetic.

A gentle cleaning with a little cotton wool moistened with water will generally remove any accumulation of wax quite satisfactorily. If when the ear is handled or squeezed there is a squelching sound, or if there is a slightly offensive smell at all, it is most probable that an infection is present in the outer ear canal. In such cases remove any matter hair around the opening to the ear canal and any discharge may then be removed with cotton wool and warm water. Foreign bodies are particularly common in the summer or autumn with dogs that are exercised in fields. The signs of a grass-seed having gained access to the outer ear canal are acute discomfort, the holding of the affected side, down, and a constant shaking of the head. The dog very rarely tries to scratch the ear in such cases as the discomfort is too great usually for this to be tolerated. It is important, if circumstances suggest such a cause, that your veterinary surgeon examine the ear, quite promptly, with a special instrument, as the sooner the offending seed or grass awn is removed the better. Under no circumstances should the ear be probed as this merely forces the seed or foreign body further down the ear canal. It may be necessary for the veterinary surgeon to administer a general anaesthetic to retrieve the offending grass-seed and therefore the animal should not be given any food at all until the examination has been made.

Pyometra or Metritis

This is an important and serious condition (pus in the womb) in which the uterus is infected. It is usually confined to maiden bitches of six years of age or more, but it is occasionally seen in young bitches as the result of infection which is usually acquired at the time of whelping or contracted even from the stud dog. In the case of the older bitch which has not been bred from, the uterine tissues begin to deteriorate in the course of time and this makes them more likely to become infected with harmful bacteria. In young bitches accidentally infected after mating, or whelping, there is no degeneration of the uterine tissues but infection occurs from outside, usually with the commoner groups of micro-organisms. All bitches should have at least one litter which will, to a large extent, prevent this very dangerous condition.

There are two main types of pyometra, the open and closed types. The latter is by far the more acute because the infection is pent up in the uterus, and there is no draining of the infected material. Accordingly the infection tends to be absorbed more rapidly into the bloodstream, producing a septicaemia. The symptoms of pyometra will vary, but a fever is almost always present, usually from 103° F. upwards; there is a loss of appetite, and a vaginal discharge in the open type is present and is usually of a brownish or pinkish colour, and as this condition becomes worse a great thirst with frequent vomiting and finally postration is seen. In cases which are not treated, a toxaemia can quickly develop particularly in the closed type and this can rapidly prove fatal if the condition is not relieved by treatment or surgery. A case of pyometra which is of the closed type may become an open type, and an open type may, on occasions, become closed, but in all instances where this condition is suspected your veterinary surgeon should be consulted, straight away. The operation for the relief of pyometra is referred to as an ovario-hysterectomy and this means that the bitch is unable to breed following the surgical removal of both the ovaries and the uterus. Where the bitch is a brood bitch or where she is very old and weak, more conservative treatment may be decided upon, and this is often successful provided it is begun at an early stage, but whatever the type of pyometra and whatever the age of the bitch, early treatment is of paramount importance.

Although pyometra can appear at more or less any time in a bitch's life, the danger period is about four to six weeks from the end of the last season, and any signs of increased thirst, slight abdominal enlargement, and other similar symptoms should be regarded as being highly suspicious of this condition.

INTERDIGITAL CYSTS

The Cocker Spaniel, owing to the large amount of hair or feathers around the feet, is perhaps more prone to this condition than many other breeds. It is usually caused initially by hair becoming caked with mud or dirt and allowing this to chafe the tender skin between the individual toes of the dog. A secondary infection occurs in the chafed area of skin and ultimately a small abscess will form between the toes. On occasions a grass-seed or barley awns can also work up in between the toes, penetrate the skin, and then produce a similar type of inflammation. Daily care of the feet is important if the dog is allowed to come into contact with mud, and this is best carried out by thoroughly washing away the mud, using a little warm water and mild soap. It is important not to use any strong antiseptics which might irritate the delicate skin. On occasions where interdigitial cysts do occur, these are best treated by a veterinary surgeon, but you can well clean and clip away the hair around the offending area before the dog is examined. Interdigital cysts can on occasions be extremely difficult to treat as the shape of the foot in certain dogs makes them more prone to this condition, and where this is the case, your veterinary surgeon would be best able to advise you on preventive measures or on actual treatment.

BAD BREATH

This is usually due to an infection of the gums and/or teeth. Dogs, as they get older, are liable to accumulate tartar on their teeth and unless this is removed, the added amounts of tartar gradually press down on the gums causing them to become inflamed and recede. When this happens, the bacteria which are normally present in the mouth and in food collect in the tartar and a foul odour is the result. Regular cleaning of the dog's teeth is almost as important as cleaning your own teeth. A soft tooth brush used once a fortnight or so should be quite adequate in keeping a dog's mouth clean. Should an accumulation of tartar already have appeared on the teeth, this should be removed by your veterinary surgeon or, if you are skilled at this task, by yourself, using a teeth scaler. Generally speaking, however, there is usually a fair degree of inflammation of the gums around the tartar-encrusted teeth and a thorough cleansing of the mouth for several days following the scaling with a little cotton wool soaked in a weak solution of a mild antiseptic, or glycerine and thymol, will usually settle this down. If, however, this should persist, then it is advisable to ask your veterinary surgeon to prescribe something more effective.

APPENDIX

BRITISH CHAMPIONS AND SHOW CHAMPIONS, 1948 to 31 July 1967

Name of Champion and Show Champion	Sex	Sire	Dam	Breeder	Owner	Date of Birth
1948: Ch. Broomleaf Bonny Lad of Shillwater	D	Blare of Broomleaf	Caroline of Shillwater	Mrs. D. H. Webb	Mrs. K. Doxford	20.10.46
Sh. Ch. Tracey Witch of Ware	B	Falconers Padlock of Ware	Whist	Miss D. Weldon	Mr. H. S. Lloyd	10.5.45
Ch. Oxshott Marxedes	D	Falconers Mark of Ware	Berrazanne of Oxshott	Mrs. K. J. Gold	Mrs. K. J. Gold	5.5.46
Ch. Golden Rule of Ide	D	Golden Rod of Ide	Ringlands Pin Up Girl	Mrs. Staff	Mr. J. H. J. Braddon	1.9.46
Ch. Rodwood Lass of Sandover	B	Falconers Mark of Ware	Mareway Marie	Mr. J. Chapman	Mr. J. H. J. Braddon	4.9.46
1949: Sh. Ch. Treetops Timber Wolf	D	Treetops Foxbar Cognac	Treetops Truly	Mrs. de Casembroot	Mrs. de Casembroot	5.8.46
Sh. Ch. Dellah Pin Up Girl	B	Augustus of Wykey	Dellah Joyful Girl	Mr. J. Blackmore	Mr. L. Page	2.7.45
Ch. Lochranza Latch Key	D	Treetops Foxbar Cognac	Lochranza Lotinga	Miss J. Macmillan	Miss J. Macmillan	2.2.47
Sh. Ch. Marcus of Akron of Ware	D	Falconers Mark of Ware	Kyra of Akron	Mr. J. C. Spiller	Mr. H. S. Lloyd	5.11.45
Ch. Harley Cherrybank Gentleman	D	Blackmoor Brand	Springbank Blue Cap	Mr. R. Roger	Mr. S. F. Topott and Mrs. G. Broadley	2.8.47

APPENDIX—continued

BRITISH CHAMPIONS AND SHOW CHAMPIONS

Name of Champion and Show Champion	Sex	Sire	Dam	Breeder	Owner	Date of Birth
Sh. Ch. Golden Valerie of Durban	B	Sixshot Willy Wagtail	Belle Maison	Mr. T. W. Malpas	Mr. J. A. Carr	5.10.46
1950: Sh. Ch. Broomleaf Black and Tan	B	B. Ch. Broomleaf Bonny Lad of Shillwater	Butterfly of Broomleaf	Mrs. K. Doxford	Mrs. K. Doxford	6.3.48
Ch. Valstar Glow of Ide	D	Blue Flash of Ide	Cobnar Mist	Mr. T. Hodgkinson	Mr. J. H. J. Braddon	27.5.48
Sh. Ch. Lochranza Lisbon Story	B	Treetops Truce	Lochranza Laughing Imp	Miss J. Macmillan	Miss J. Macmillan	14.6.47
Ch. Colinwood Son of a Gun	D	Colinwood Roughrider	Downpour of Dondeau	Mr. H. D. P. Becker	Mr. A. W. Collins	26.3.48
Sh. Ch. Joywyns Blueboy of Ware	D	Fantee Silver Sentinel	Cartret Charmer	Miss J. Ruben	Mr. H. S. Lloyd	7.4.49
1951: Sh. Ch. Blue Flint of Ide	D	Harley Sandylands Flare	Falconers Fuchsia	Mrs. E. K. Dugeon	Mr. J. H. J. Braddon	11.7.48
Sh. Ch. Broomleaf Primula of Kenevon	B	Sixshot Willy Wagtail	Kenevon Bran of Broomleaf	Mrs. Barnes	Mrs. K. Doxford	12.12.46
Sh. Ch. Treetops Tender	B	Treetops Tenant	Mimosa of Dorswick	Mrs. Wicks	Mrs. W. de Casembroot	12.7.46
Sh. Ch. Valstar Willow	B	Colinwood Cowboy	Cobnar Mist	Mr. T. Hodgkinson	Mr. F. Duke	7.9.47
Sh. Ch. Pennoncelle of Oxshott	B	Oxshott Penndarcye	Reeta of Oxshott	Mrs. V. Fisher	Mrs. K. J. Gold	20.7.47

Name of Champion and Show Champion	Sex	Sire	Dam	Breeder	Owner	Date of Birth
Sh. Ch. Sixshot Woodywoodpecker	D	Sixshot Willy Wagtail	Sixshot Nightingale	Mrs. V. Lucas-Lucas	Mrs. V. Lucas-Lucas	18.9.48
Sh. Ch. Golden Star of Ulwell	D	Sixshot Willy Wagtail	Romance of Ulwell	Mrs. D. Garrington	Mrs. D. Garrington	10.4.46
Sh. Ch. Sunkist Lotus Lily	B	Golden Rule of Ide	Crocus of Aingarth	Mr. J. Lindsay	Mr. & Mrs. D. Mackenzie	8.5.48
1952: Sh. Ch. Scarcroft Georgiana of Rafborn	B	Ahmed of Scarcroft	Super Black	Mr. S. B. Asquith	Sq. Ldr. & Mrs. J. D. Hill	17.5.48
Sh. Ch. Craigomus Critic of Ide	D	Golden Rule of Ide	Crocus of Aingarth	Mr. J. H. J. Braddon	Mr. J. H. J. Braddon	8.5.48
Sh. Ch. Jaycee Marxedeson	D	Oxshott Marxedes	Jaycee Motala Turquoise	Mr. J. H. Connolly	Mr. J. H. Connolly	1.6.49
Sh. Ch. Bonny Lass of Kenavon	B	Broomleaf Bonny Lad of Shillwater	Bramble of Kenavon	Miss B. M. Mingay	Miss B. M. Mingay	4.3.48
Sh. Ch. Witchdoctor of Ware	D	Falconers Mark of Ware	Tracey Witch of Ware	Mr. H. S. Lloyd	Mr. H. S. Lloyd	25.10.50
Sh. Ch. Broomleaf Ballet Shoes	B	Broomleaf Kim of Churdles	Brown Bess of Broomleaf	Miss G. Anslow	Mrs. K. Doxford	28.5.50
Ch. Talwrn Riverbank Rainmaker	B	Harley Riverbank Recall	Riverbank Regina	Mrs. G. L. Thomas	Mrs. J. Rothwell	25.2.50
Sh. Ch. Courtdale China Model	B	Ronfil Regent	Polly of Halford	Mrs. I. C. Burford	Mrs. S. G. Jones	29.6.50
Ch. Domino of Ide	D	Blue Flash of Ide	Rodwood Lass of Sandover	Mr. J. H. J. Braddon	Mr. J. H. J. Braddon	26.5.51

APPENDIX—continued

BRITISH CHAMPIONS AND SHOW CHAMPIONS

Name of Champion and Show Champion	Sex	Sire	Dam	Breeder	Owner	Date of Birth
1953: Sh. Ch. Ronfil Regent	D	Colinwood Cowboy	Dream Delight	Mrs. T. M. Bebb	Mrs. T. M. Bebb	12.10.48
Sh. Ch. Bramlyn Sunflower	B	Treetops Truce	Bramlyn Brown Sugar	Mrs. M. H. Bowden	Mrs. M. Mather	21.8.49
Sh. Ch. Ernocroft Expert	D	Ernocroft Highlandie Laddie	Ernocroft Evenmist	Miss D. Whitehead	Mrs. E. Coulton and Mr. D. Kershaw	22.10.49
Ch. Colinwood Haybury Howitzer	D	Colinwood Son of a Gun	Haybury Hushabye	Lady Helen Berry	Mr. A. W. Collins	2.3.50
Sh. Ch. Derrydale Duskie	B	Ernocroft Expert	Treetops Sheba of Woodlands	Mrs. M. Bullivant	Mrs. M. Bullivant	25.5.51
Ch. Solinda of Traquair	B	Broomleaf Bonny Lad of Shillwater	Sweet Sue of Traquair	Mr. R. Kaye-Walker	Mr. R. H. Wylde	16.6.48
Sh. Ch. Sixshot Sugar Bird	B	Sixshot Willy Wagtail	Dorswick Love in a Mist	Mrs. H. C. Wicks	Mrs. V. Lucas-Lucas	19.6.51
Sh. Ch. Treetops Trader	D	Treetops Foxbar Cognac	Treetops Trillion	Mrs. W. de Casembroot	Mrs. W. de Casembroot	15.12.49
Sh. Ch. Blue Queen of Ide	B	Blue Flash of Ide	Blue Gown of Ide	Mr. A. E. Morris	Mr. J. H. J. Braddon	1.5.52
Sh. Ch. Lochranza Eldwythe's Enchanter	B	Lochranza Latchkey	Solinda of Traquair	Mr. R. H. Wylde	Miss J. Macmillan	16.10.51
1954: Sh. Ch. Colinwood Jessely Journeyman	D	Colinwood Cowboy	Pierette of Jessely	Mrs. M. V. Jessup	Mr. A. W. Collins	21.7.52

Name of Champion and Show Champion	Sex	Sire	Dam	Breeder	Owner	Date of Birth
Sh. Ch. Springbank Silver Flame	B	Springbank Covenmore Silver Flare	Springbank Trudy	Mr. W. Sunderland	Miss V. Ferguson	22.7.52
Sh. Ch. Weirdene Learig Annitra	B	Aberthaw Commander of Reaghbel	Learig Ladybird	Miss J. Donaldson	Mr. J. Auld	26.6.50
Ch. Colinwood Firebrand	D	Colinwood Cowboy	Pierette of Jessely	Mrs. M. V. Jessup	Mr. A. W. Collins	20.3.51
Ch. Dennydene Dousonne of Ide	D	Carwyns Shandy	Ravensclough Twilight	Mrs. G. M. Briston	Mr. J. H. J. Braddon	19.9.52
1955: Sh. Ch. Nostrebor Nightlight	B	Nostrebor Hillrise Hilray	Nostrebor National	Mrs. E. S. Robertson	Mrs. E. S. Robertson	1.9.51
Sh. Ch. Sixshot Storm Bird	D	Sixshot Woody Woodpecker	Sixshot Cuckoo	Mrs. V. Lucas-Lucas	Mrs. V. Lucas-Lucas	5.7.52
Sh. Ch. Colinwood Black Sombrero	D	Colinwood Gamekeeper	Colinwood Chance Step	Mr. A. W. Collins	Mr. A. W. Collins	27.2.53
Ch. Nostrebor Riverbank Rogue	D	Harley Riverbank Recall	Riverbank Regina	Mrs. G. L. Thomas	Mrs. E. S. Robertson	26.7.52
Sh. Ch. Glendorgal Spritely Lad	D	Marcus of Akron of Ware	Salwood Sprite	Mr. & Mrs. D. G. Brewer	Mrs. L. M. Brewer	5.10.49
Sh. Ch. Goldenfields Merry Maiden	B	Mantop Merry Legs	Goldenfield Merry Miss	Miss D. Robinson	Miss D. Robinson	11.11.52
Sh. Ch. Merryworth Matches	B	Colinwood Firebrand	Merryworth Magical	Mrs. E. F. Chadwick	Mrs. E. F. Chadwick	13.1.54

BRITISH CHAMPIONS AND SHOW CHAMPIONS

Name of Champion and Show Champion	Sex	Sire	Dam	Breeder	Owner	Date of Birth
Sh. Ch. Cassa Cristina	B	Rivoli Watmor Coppersmith	Cassa Crisp	Mesdames E. Coulton and D. Kershaw	Mesdames E. Coulton and D. Kershaw	29.10.51
Sh. Ch. Treetops Walkie Talkie	D	Treetops Trade	Treetops Tiller Girl	Mrs. W. de Casembroot	Mrs. W. de Casembroot	27.6.53
Sh. Ch. Betrothal of Broomleaf	B	Broomleaf Bonny Lad of Shillwater	Broomleaf Primula of Kenavon	Mrs. K. Doxford	Mrs. K. Doxford	2.6.50
Sh. Ch. Wendayle Valjolie of Misbourne	B	Pickpocket of Misbourne	Wendayle Valetta	Mrs. D. M. Cole	Miss D. M. Hahn	12.7.53
Sh. Ch. Lady Caradon of Ide	B	Colinwood Roughrider	Ardenoak Starshine	Mr. L. Hughes	Mr. J. H. J. Braddon	9.11.52
Sh. Ch. Pickpocket of Misbourne	D	Broomleaf Bonny Lad of Shillwater	Swanette of Misbourne	Miss D. M. Hahn	Miss D. M. Hahn	1.5.52
1956: Sh. Ch. Gatehampton Jennifer	B	Lochranza Eldwythe's Earl	Gatehampton Silver Cloud	Mrs. A. L. Cloke	Mrs. A. L. Cloke	23.4.53
Sh. Ch. Treetops Tudor Queen	B	Treetops Trigger Happy	Treetops Tilda	Mrs. P. Price	Mrs. W. de Casembroot	3.7.53
Sh. Ch. Darnmill Dolly Blue	B	Joywyns Blue Boy of Ware	Darnmill Buryhill Pipistrelle	Mrs. E. Cunningham	Mrs. E. Cunningham	12.9.52
Sh. Ch. Bartonblount Doublesix	D	Blue Flash of Ide	Dollishill Merry Minx	Mrs. T. W. Mellor	Mr. G. Brooks	22.2.53
Sh. Ch. Cassa Chance	B	Sixshot Woody	Roscott Susie	Mrs. L. Barringer	Mrs. D. Kershaw	26.1.54

Name of Champion and Show Champion	Sex	Sire	Dam	Breeder	Owner	Date of Birth
Sh. Ch. Gatehampton Dumbo	D	Broomleaf Ernocroft Event	Gatehampton Sun Rise	Mrs. A. L. Cloke	Mrs. A. L. Cloke	20.6.53
Ch. Colinwood Silver Lariot	D	Joywyns Blue Flash	Truslers Misty Morn	Miss H. M. Allan	Mr. A. J. Collins	26.8.54
Sh. Ch. Broomleaf Camellia of Dorswick	B	Sixshot Woody Woodpecker	Honeysuckle of Dorswick	Mrs. H. C. Wicks	Mrs. K. Doxford	18.12.52
1957: Sh. Ch. Cassa Contessa	B	Ernocroft Esquire	Cassa Cristina	Mrs. D. Kershaw	Mrs. D. Kershaw	27.10.54
Sh. Ch. Noslien Nola	B	Noslien Nickel Coin	Lass of Carrick	Miss I. S. Johnston	Miss P. Neilson	24.12.54
Sh. Ch. Golden Wagson of Ulwell	D	Goldenstar of Ulwell	Olicana Caramel of Ulwell	Mrs. D. Garrington	Mrs. D. Garrington	29.6.53
Ch. Lucklena Musical Maid	B	Domino of Ide	Lucklena Melodious Maid	Mr. A. S. Mansfield	Mr. A. S. Mansfield	7.11.55
Sh. Ch. Falconers Herald of Ware	D	Thornfalcon Fanfare of Ware	Falconers Brenda of Ware	Mr. H. S. Lloyd	Mr. H. S. Lloyd	15.3.56
Sh. Ch. Colinwood Outrider	D	Colinwood Firebrand	Truslers Tracery	Miss H. M. Allan	Mr. A. W. Collins	11.2.54
Sh. Ch. Silver Cloud of Ormeau of Ware	B	Colinwood Cobbler	Crofthill Cascade	Mr. J. Duncan	Miss J. Lloyd	18.6.56
Sh. Ch. Dellah Merrymaker of Wykey	D	Joywyns Blue Boy of Ware	Dellah Merry Maid of Wykey	Mrs. N. Basnett-Broughhall	Mr. & Mrs. D. L. Page	27.4.55
1958: Ch. Lochdene Lac d'Amour	B	Talwrn Pia Gynt	Broomleaf Bright Budget	Mrs. P. G. Tosh	Mrs. P. G. Tosh	5.6.55

APPENDIX—*continued*

BRITISH CHAMPIONS AND SHOW CHAMPIONS

Name of Champion and Show Champion	Sex	Sire	Dam	Breeder	Owner	Date of Birth
Sh. Ch. Broomleaf Black-eyed Susan	B	Billy Budd of Broomleaf	Bubbley of Broomleaf	Miss K. Doxford	Mrs. K. Doxford	19.10.55
Sh. Ch. Winter Harvest of Weirdene	D	Aust. Ch. Wings-ashore of Weirdene	Weirdene Trech Zenda	Mr. R. Weir	Mr. E. Weir	10.10.57
1959: Valjoker of Misbourne	D	Sixshot The Black Cockatoo	Sh. Ch. Wendayle Valjolie of Misbourne	Miss D. Hahn	Miss D. Hahn	11.1.57
Sh. Ch. Buryhill Cedar	D	Valstar Glow of Ide	Sh. Ch. Darnmill Dolly Blue	Mrs. E. Cunningham	Mrs. A. Woolley	3.9.54
Sh. Ch. Tideway Cabin Boy of Eastlands	D	Ch. Colinwood Silver Lariot	Tideway Hightide of Eastlands	Mrs D. P. Shakes-peare	Mrs. M. Harrison	29.7.56
1960: Sh. Ch. Sixshot Shorelark	B	Sh. Ch. Sixshot Stormbird	Sixshot Moorhen	Mrs. V. Lucas-Lucas	Mrs. V. Lucas-Lucas	31.3.56
Sh. Ch. Broomleaf Boots and Shoes	D	Bootboy of Broomleaf	Sh. Ch. Broomleaf Ballet Shoes	Mrs. K. Doxford	Mrs. K. Doxford	27.10.56
Sh. Ch. Colinwood Cobler	D	Colinwood Jester of Glenbogie	Colinwood Silver Slipper	Miss P. N. Collins	Mr. J. Auld	16.2.54
Sh. Ch. Wake Early of Weirdene	B	Colinwood Singing Cowboy	Weirdene Learigg Annitra	Mr. J. Auld	Mr. Richmond Weir	10.6.56
Sh. Ch. Astrawin Aphrodite	B	Sixshot The Black Cockatoo	Astrawin Arabesque	Mr. & Mrs. S. V. Wise	Mr. & Mrs. S. V. Wise	8.6.57

Name of Champion and Show Champion	Sex	Sire	Dam	Breeder	Owner	Date of Birth
Sh. Ch. Tangee of Tolstem	B	Lochranza London Tan	Tango of Scarlac	Mrs. O. Birch	Mrs. O. Birch	2.2.56
1961: Sh. Ch. Sixshot Otto the Owl	D	Sh. Ch. Sixshot Woody Woodpecker	Sh. Ch. Sixshot Sugar Bird	Mrs. V. Lucas-Lucas	Mrs. V. Lucas-Lucas	30.11.57
Sh. Ch. Atway My Love of Misbourne	B	Sh. Ch. Valjoker of Misbourne	Black Nun of Atway	Miss A. Gurney	Miss D. Hahn	4.7.58
Sh. Ch. Gay Domino of Ide	D	Ch. Domino of Ide	Gay Time of Ide	Mr. J. H. Braddon	Mr. J. H. Braddon	11.6.58
1962: Sh. Ch. Colinwood Morning Star	B	Sh. Ch. Colinwood Silver Lariot	Colinwood Venus	Mrs. G. M. Champion	Mr. A. W. Collins	31.12.58
Sh. Ch. Lochranza Dancing Master	D	Lochranza Exceed	Lochranza Dancing Shoes	Miss J. Coull	Miss J. MacMillan	22.12.57
Sh. Ch. Silver Mogul of Hearts	D	Sh. Ch. Colinwood Silver Lariot	Sh. Ch. Lucklena Musical Maid	Mr. A. S. Mansfield	Mr. T. Hubert Arthur	13.8.58
Sh. Ch. Wells Fargo of Weirdene	D	Weirdene Barnscour Fisher	Weirdene Trech of Zenda	Mr. Richmond Weir	Mr. Richmond Weir	17.11.59
Sh. Ch. Colinwood Cheyenne	D	Sh. Ch. Colinwood Silver Lariot	Sh. Ch. Creighleith Geisha Girl	Mrs. M. Robinson	Mr. A. W. Collins	10.7.58
Sh. Ch. Lochranza Floral Dancer	B	Sh. Ch. Lochranza Dancing Master	Lochranza Lusaka	Miss J. MacMillan	Miss J. MacMillan	2.2.59
Sh. Ch. Winter Yana of Weirdene	B	Sh. Ch. Winter Harvest of Weirdene	Lochranza High Trees Orange Petal	Mr. T. Thomson	Mr. Richmond Weir	28.4.59

APPENDIX—continued

BRITISH CHAMPIONS AND SHOW CHAMPIONS

Name of Champion and Show Champion	Sex	Sire	Dam	Breeder	Owner	Date of Birth
Sh. Ch. Merryworth Musical Box	D	Sh. Ch. Colinwood Silver Lariot	Merryworth Music	Mrs. E. Chadwick	Mrs. E. Chadwick	14.9.58
Sh. Ch. Craigleith Cinderella	B	Goldenfields Minstral Boy	Creigleith Heathermaid	Mrs. M. Robinson	Mrs. M. Robinson	23.12.59
Sh. Ch. Miss Julie of Jaycee	B	Dellah Merrymaker of Wykey	Penny Piece of Jaycee	Mr. J. H. Connolly	Mrs. J. H. Connolly	11.7.59
Sh. Ch. Shooting Star of Hearts	D	Sh. Ch. Colinwood Silver Lariot	Sh. Ch. Lucklena Musical Maid	Mr. A. S. Mansfield	Mrs. Hubert Arthur	13.8.58
1963: Sh. Ch. Lochranza Hightrees Red Admiral	D	Sh. Ch. Lochranza Dancing Master	Hightrees Sunflower	Mrs. Ridout	Miss J. Macmillan	14.8.61
Sh. Ch. Glencora	D	Sixshot The Black Cockatoo	Sh. Ch. Black Jade of Lochnell	Mr. J. Auld	Mr. J. Auld	30.4.61
Sh. Ch. Glencora Generous Gift	B	Black Cocade of Lochnell	Why Chance of Weirdene	Mr. R. Weis	Mr. J. Auld	7.5.61
1964: Sh. Ch. Astrawin Aphrodite	B	Sixshot The Black Cockatoo	Astrawin Arabesque	Mr. & Mrs. Wise	Mr. & Mrs. Wise	8.6.57
Sh. Ch. Carmabar Glenharrie	D	Carmabar Garry	Carmabar Donna Dimple	Mrs. Caffyn	Mrs. Clarke	24.10.60
Sh. Ch. Colinwood Bunting	B	Sh. Ch. Valjoker of Misbourne	Colinwood Moorhen	Mr. Griffin	Miss Collins	8.26.60
Sh. Ch. Crosbeian Thornfalcon Flamenco	B	Ch. Colinwood Silver Lariot	Thornfalcon Blue Frosting	Miss Seymour Nichols	Mrs. Trench	27.9.59

Name of Champion and Show Champion	Sex	Sire	Dam	Breeder	Owner	Date of Birth
Sh. Ch. Crackshill Alpine Crocus of Kenavon	B	Sh. Ch. Lochranza Merryleaf Eigar	Crackshill Tawny Toes	Miss Richie	Miss Mingay	15.8.62
Sh. Ch. Gatehampton Black Sambo of Lochnell	D	Red Bracken of Lochnell	Kirkdon Hazari Harosa	Mr. Heavisides	Mrs. Cloke	16.5.62
Sh. Ch. Glencora Gallant Star	D	Colinwood Texan	Glencora Treasure	Mr. Auld	Mr. Auld	8.5.60
Sh. Ch. Glencora Generous Gift	B	Black Cockade of Lochnell	Why Chance of Weirdene	Mr. Weir	Mr. Auld	7.5.61
Sh. Ch. Lochranza Hightrees Red Admiral	D	Sh. Ch. Lochranza Dancing Master	Hightrees Sunflower	Mrs. Ridout	Miss Macmillan	4.7.61
Sh. Ch. Moyhill Miss Jazz	B	Sh. Ch. Colinwood Cobler	Moyhill Wisegirl of Kilbride	Messrs. Cudworth and Fletcher	Messrs. Cudworth and Fletcher	12.6.59
Sh. Ch. Peasemore Pirouette	B	Thornfalcon Foxtrot	Colinwood Blue Lace	Miss Annetts	Miss Annetts	21.1.59
Sh. Ch. Quettadene Lucky Dip	B	Sh. Ch. Valjoker of Misbourne	Quettadene Jolly Whisper	Mrs. Woodbridge	Mrs. Woodbridge	26.7.61
Sh. Ch. Ronfil Remembrance	B	Courtdale Colinwood Seahawk	Ronfil Courtdale Royal Doulton	Mrs. Bebb	Mrs. Bebb	10.11.61
Sh. Ch. Segedunum Aide de Camp	D	Merryworth Muleteer	Saddlebow Gerda	Mr. McCullum	Mr. Stalker	24.12.60
Sh. Ch. Shooting Star of Hearts	D	Ch. Colinwood Silver Lariot	Ch. Lucklena Musical Maid	Mr. Mansfield	Mr. Hubert Arthur	13.8.58

BRITISH CHAMPIONS AND SHOW CHAMPIONS

Name of Champion and Show Champion	Sex	Sire	Dam	Breeder	Owner	Date of Birth
Sh. Ch. Sixshot Dan The Duck	D	Sh. Ch. Sixshot Storm Bird	Sixshot Garden Warbler	Mrs. Lucas-Lucas	Mrs. Lucas Lucas	15.1.63
Sh. Ch. Weirdene Questing Strathspey	D	Weirdene Questing Solitaire	Questing Beryl	Dr. Burns	Mr. R. Weir	4.8.61
Sh. Ch. Wells Fargo of Weirdene	D	Weirdene Barnscar Fisher	Weirdene Trech Zenda	Mr. R. Weir	Mr. R. Weir	17.11.59
1965: Sh. Ch. Astrawin Amusing	B	Sh. Ch. Valjoker of Misbourne	Astrawin Artemis	Mr. & Mrs. Wise	Mr. & Mrs. Wise	19.4.63
Sh. Ch. Cochise Circe	B	Sh. Ch. Wells Fargo of Weirdene	Conehise Chiyoko	Lt. Cdr. & Mrs. Blake	Lt. Cdr. & Mrs. Blake	1.6.63
Sh. Ch. Courtdale Flag Lieutenant	D	Courtdale Colinwood Seahawk	Courtdale Kinkelbridge Gina	Mrs. Anstey	Mrs. Jones	3.1.63
Sh. Ch. Donvale Demara	B	Colinwood Tenderfoot	Donvale Delia	Mr. H. Hubbard	Mr. H. Hubbard	25.8.62
Sh. Ch. Eldwythe Mornessa Milora	B	Sh. Ch. Lochranza Dancing Master	Eldwythe Elza	Mr. & Mrs. Greenaway	Mrs. M. France	11.7.62
Sh. Ch. Glencora Black Ace	D	Sixshot The Black Cockatoo	Sh. Ch. Black Jade of Lochnell	Mr. J. Auld	Mr. J. Auld	30.4.61
Sh. Ch. Goldenfields Geisha Girl	B	Can. Ch. Craigleith Vagabond King	Goldenfields Starlet	Miss D. Robinson	Miss D. Robinson	27.9.61
Sh. Ch. Lochdene Pepper Pot	B	Sh. Ch. Glencora Black Ace	Lochdene Bubble Gum	Mrs. P. Tosh	Mrs. P. Tosh	23.5.62

Name of Champion and Show Champion	Sex	Sire	Dam	Breeder	Owner	Date of Birth
Sh. Ch. Lochranza Quettadene Marksman	D	Sh. Ch. Lochranza Dancing Master	Quettadene Prudence	Mrs. Woodbridge	Miss J. Macmillan	8.10.62
Sh. Ch. Quettadene Mark	D	Sh. Ch. Lochranza Merryleaf Eigar	Quettadene Prudence	Mrs. Woodbridge	Mrs. Woodbridge and D. L. Page	28.6.64
Sh. Ch. Saffron of Settnor	B	Dorna Dambuster	Courtdale Blue Willow	Mrs. J. Owen	Mrs. J. Owen	13.11.62
Sh. Ch. Topbrands Blue Prince	D	Friesian Lad	Topbrands Sylvaqueen	Mr. L. Alsop	Mr. L. Alsop	18.11.61
Sh. Ch. Westside Story of Weirdene	B	Black Cockade of Locknell	Aust. Ch. Why Chance of Weirdene	Mr. R. Weir	Mr. R. Weir	7.5.61
1966: Sh. Ch. Astrawin April Fire	D	Sh. Ch. Lochranza Merryleaf Eigar	Astrawin April Flame	Mr. & Mrs. Wise	Mr. & Mrs. Wise	4.7.63
Sh. Ch. Blackbird of Broomleaf	D	Sh. Ch. Lochranza Merryleaf Eigar	Sh. Ch. Broomleaf Black Eyed Susan	Mrs. Doxford	Mrs. Doxford	21.11.62
Sh. Ch. Colinwood Jackdaw of Lochnell	D	Sh. Ch. Blackbird of Broomleaf	Lochranza Red Sash of Lochnell	Mrs. Cameron	Miss Collins	2.5.64
Sh. Ch. Craigleith Maggie May	B	Sh. Ch. Wells Fargo of Weirdene	Craigleth Princess Ida	Mrs. Robinson	Mrs. Robinson	19.7.64
Sh. Ch. Lochranza Darnclever	D	Sh. Ch. Lochranza Hightrees Red Admiral	Lochranza Dancing Lesson	Miss Macmillan and Miss Coull	Miss Macmillan and Miss Coull	27.3.64
Sh. Ch. Val of Lochnell	D	Valentine of Lochnell	Alexandra of Lochnell	Mrs. Cameron	Mrs. Cameron	30.10.61

BRITISH CHAMPIONS AND SHOW CHAMPIONS

Name of Champion and Show Champion	Sex	Sire	Dam	Breeder	Owner	Date of Birth
Sh. Ch. Lucklena Musical Director	D	Ch. Colinwood Silver Lariot	Ch. Lucklena Musical Maid	Mr. Mansfield	Mr. Mansfield	14.11.61
Sh. Ch. Nosliem Naughty Nineties	B	Sh. Ch. Lochranza Dancing Master	Nosliem Nainsook	Mrs. & Miss Neilson	Mrs. & Miss Neilson	25.11.60
Sh. Ch. Quettadene Dream Awhile	B	Sh. Ch. Lochranza Merryleaf Eigar	Quettadene Prudence	Mrs. Woodbridge	Mrs. Woodbridge	5.1.163
1967 (to 31 July): Sh. Ch. Broomleaf of Thulemoor Tulip	B	Treetops Top Bid	Thulemoor Darling Bud	Mrs. Merton	Mrs. Doxford	10.7.63
Sh. Ch. Gatehampton Lochranza Fascination	B	Lochranza Honey Bean	Lochranza Caramel	Miss Macmillan	Mrs. Cloke	25.10.65
Sh. Ch. Nostrebor Nonchalant	B	Freshet Florin of Quatford	Minnon of Quatford	Mrs. Parker Smith	Mrs. Robertson	15.8.65
Sh. Ch. Platonstown Lovely Cottage	B	Sh. Ch. Lochranza Merryleaf Eigar	Patbarossa Unity	Mrs. Snary	Mrs. Snary	9.8.63
Sh. Ch. Winning Ways of Weirdene	B	Rockstone Rambler	Questing Sapphire	Miss Bartlett	Mr. Weir	22.6.64

INDEX